NEW WRITING AND WRITERS XVI

NEW WRITING AND WRITERS
16

by

William Burroughs, Dino Buzzati, David Craig,
Elspeth Davie, Ingeborg Drewitz, Kathleen Greenwood,
Maryon Jeane, Neil Jordan, Sarah Lawson,
B.C. Leale, Sarah McCoy, Michael Moorcock

JOHN CALDER
LONDON

This collection first published in hardback and paperback editions in
Great Britain, 1979, by John Calder (Publishers) Ltd.,
18 Brewer Street, London W1R 4AS
and in a hardback edition in the U.S.A. by
Humanities Press Inc., Atlantic Highlands, New Jersey 07716
and in a paperback edition in the U.S.A. by riverrun press Inc.,
4951 Top Line Drive, Dallas, Texas 75247

Some of the poems by Sarah Lawson have previously appeared in
Counterpoint and *Orbis*.
Some of the poems by B.C. Leale have previously appeared in the
following magazines: *Ambit, Anthill, Bone Whistle, Ipso Facto, Montana
Gothic, Poetry Survey, Slow Dancer* and *Tribune*.
THE KASSANDRA PENINSULA, since revised, was first published in
Game magazine.

The Publishers gratefully acknowledge financial assistance from the Arts
Council of Great Britain.

Photoset in 11/11pt Baskerville by Specialised Offset Services Ltd., Liverpool
Printed by M. & A. Thomson Litho Ltd., East Kilbride
Bound by Hunter & Foulis Ltd., Edinburgh, Scotland

CONTENTS

INTRODUCTION

The 16th edition of *NWW* returns to the larger format of *NWW 13* and *14* with twelve contributors from six different countries: Canada, Germany, Ireland, Italy, the U.K. and the U.S.A. Designed originally as a series to promote the best international new writers it has, since *NWW 13*, juxtaposed new writers with shorter work by established authors that might otherwise have only been published in a more ephemeral form.

William Burroughs is one of the most important post-war writers, whose novel, *The Naked Lunch*, and the books which followed has radically altered the way we perceive and write about the world: the impact of the 'cut-up' and 'fold-in' techniques, pioneered by William Burroughs and Brion Gysin and explained in their forthcoming book *The Third Mind*, has affected writers of all kinds and nationalities. 'Cobble Stone Gardens', a short prose text published in England for the first time, combines photographs with words and a tightly controlled use of the 'fold-in' technique to produce a powerful, polemical elegy. Michael Moorcock is another writer whose fine disregard for conventional categories and forms has produced some of the most exciting new writing to come out of the fusion between science fiction fantasy and experimental fiction: a fusion that has already produced novels such as those by Kurt Vonnegut, J.G. Ballard and William Burroughs. Moorcock's latest book, *Gloriana* is an extraordinarily elaborate yet serious fantasy which he describes as a 'romance' that 'while it is neither an "Elizabethan Fantasia" nor an historical novel ... does have some relation to *The Faerie Queene*.' 'The Kassandra Peninsula' features Una Persson, who, he says, has somewhat taken over from Jerry Cornelius in his shorter pieces and who will be the heroine of his next project.

There are extracts from new work by two very different novelists. Sarah McCoy, whose novel *Dead and Gone*, clearly influenced by the ideas and techniques of *nouveau romanciers*, is concerned not only with the inner life but with the life and ultimate sovereignty of the text itself. Neil Jordan is one of the founder members of the Irish Writers' Co-Operative, currently the most exciting publishing house in Ireland, and while his style is *apparently* more conventional, he is no less aware of the problems of writing fiction today. The climax of the finished book is planned as an apocalyptic meeting of past and present, and in these two extracts we see the careful creation of two of the main characters: characters pushed beyond the bounds of their persons, so that neither of them (any more than the other characters including the narrator himself) is self-contained: they extend into everything they have ever touched and thought about, each of them is the creation of the other and in the end of the narrator's imaginings.

The stories published here show the vitality that the short story has always had. The range is wide, from Dino Buzzati's moral fantasies, through the meticulously created story, 'Change of Face', by Elspeth Davie; the strange, shocking power of David Craig's 'I Didn't Know what he Meant' (the story of a young Scottish girl's total incomprehension in the face of parental duplicity and the nature of sexuality); Ingeborg Drewitz's account of a murder in which the narrator (a writer) suspects from the start who the murderer is; to Kathleen Greenwood's two dazzling stories, whose stylistic facility lures the reader into contact with her substantial themes of time, memory and consciousness.

There is a great deal of excellent poetry being written at the moment and not just by established poets – such as Seamus Heaney, Brian Patten, Ted Hughes, Geoffrey Hill, Philip Larkin or Peter Porter, in the U.K. and Ireland for example – but by others who are not at all well known. One of the main problems for these poets is the difficulty they encounter in gaining a wider readership and recognition than that provided by single poem appearances in magazines and anthologies. The images in Maryon Jeane's poems have a limpid accuracy which is controlled by the overall structure so that personal emotion gains the reader's attention without self-seeking clamour. The American born Sarah Lawson, who now lives in England, has an ability to create dramatic tension that liberates an understated, penetrating humour which is at its best in 'Giotto' and 'Gravel Paths in Kentucky'. B.C. Leale's literary associations begin with the latter days of 'the Group' and he is one of the few British poets to have absorbed and developed the influences of Dada and Surrealism, as can be clearly seen not only in his humorous 'Homage to Marcel Duchamp/Rrose Sélavy' but also in the startling juxtaposition of images in poems like 'The Trapping of K', 'A Dream of the Film Luis Buñuel nearly Made' or 'Visible Wildnotes', while other aspects of his extensive range are shown in his poems on music and the sequence on Constable.

The contents of *NWW 16* are as varied as ever and give, we hope, a good idea of some of the latest developments in International writing, as well as drawing attention to writers who have not as yet penetrated the still restrictive climate of British publishing.

The Publishers

I
COBBLE STONE GARDENS

Willliam Burroughs

Photograph by G· ard Malanga

Since the arrival of *The Naked Lunch*, one of the key books of the post-war period, the work of William Burroughs has come to be seen as a brilliant demonstration of the relation of language to consciousness. Norman Mailer has said that he thinks 'William Burroughs is the only American novelist writing today who may be possessed by genius.' Starting with *Junky* in 1953, written under the pen-name of William Lee, he has in a series of powerful novels including *The Soft Machine, The Ticket that Exploded, The Wild Boys* and *Exterminator!* (all published in England by Calder & Boyars) confronted the twentieth century and particularly America with its own image. In the introduction to *The Naked Lunch* he writes 'As always the lunch is naked. If civilised countries want to return to Druid Hanging Rites in the Sacred Grove or to drink blood with Aztecs and feed their gods with the blood of human sacrifice, let them see what they actually eat and drink. Let them see what is on the end of that long newspaper spoon.' His most recent book *Ah Pook is Here and Other Texts* (John Calder), which includes *The Book of Breeething* and *Electronic Revolution*, further explores these themes: he is currently working on a new novel to be called *Cities of the Red Night*. William Burroughs was born in St Louis in 1914 and graduated from Harvard. Formerly a news reporter, private detective and exterminator, he served with the AUS in World War II. After a long stay in England he returned to the U.S.A. at the end of the sixties.

COBBLE STONE GARDENS

Dedicated to the memory of
my mother and father –

*We never know how much we learn
From those who never will return.*

Edward Arlington Robinson
from *The Man Flamonde*

Laura Lee Burroughs

Pershing Avenue St Louis Missouri in the 1920's ... Red brick three-story houses, lawns in front, large back yards with gardens separated by high wooden fences overgrown with morning glory and rose vines and at the back of the yard an ash pit and no one from Sanitation sniffing around in those days.

At that time the River of the Fathers was one of the sights and smells of St Louis though not exactly a tourist attraction. The River des Peres was a vast open sewer that meandered through the city ... I remember as a child with my young cousin standing on its grassy banks and watching as turds shot out into the yellow water from vents along the sides.

'Hey looky ... someone just did it.'

During the summer months the smell of shit and coal gas permeated the city, bubbling up from the river's murky depths to cover the oily iridescent surface with miasmal mists. I liked this smell myself, but there was talk of sealing it in and sullen mutters of revolt from the peasantry: 'My teenage daughters is cunt deep in shit. Is this the American way of life?'

I thought so and I didn't want it changed. Personally I found it most charming drinking Whistle on the back porch, blue mist and gas light in the hot summer night ... the smell of coal gas from the river which ran just at the bottom of our garden beyond the ash pit. One night I was sitting there with my sensitive inspirational old maid school teacher I borrowed from Tennessee Williams. She raised alligators from tiny babies and released them in the river to fight off the sanitation men, and she had a vicious five-foot alligator ready in her basement. She called him Yummy – wouldn't you if he was protecting your way of life?

'How I hate them!' she exclaimed. I had never heard her use the word before and I was shocked but she went on, oblivious ... 'Those bastards from Sanitation sniffing round my ash pit.' Fire flies in the garden, a smell of gardenias and sewage ... she suddenly gripped my arm. 'We must keep all this. The old family creatures need this smell to breathe in.'

She drew her hands together and looked up at the frayed stars.

By now every citizen has got himself up to look like a cop and there are vast roving bands of vigilantes with their own jails and courts. Here's a cop retired to his farm. He paces up and down. He can't stand it. He grabs his badge and gun and erupts into the street where elegantly-dressed citizens parade up and down – backdrop is Palm Beach, Newport, Saratoga, Palm Springs. The cop is seeing an old western. Bandits are robbing the bank. He draws and fires with deadly accuracy. A bank president grunts and slides to the pavement. Six shots and six bandits lay dead. The mayor himself is coming to congratulate him. And who is that on the bank president's phantom arm? None other than his gilt-edged daughter. The lawman goes all bashful when he sees her, showing his teeth in little dog smiles like Gary Cooper when he is being a cute millionaire.

'Put that nut in a straitjacket' snarls the Director. 'He has loused up our take.'

'And destroyed the upper crust of our town' say the little peoples plaintively.

'You extras make me sick. The studio pays you thirty cools a day. What you want to do? Get as rich as I am? ... Hello ... what's that? Studio security has revolted and seized the Southeast Wing? Put me through to Paramount ...'

Line went dead. The film is running out by the twilight's last gleamings. One push and it went down like a house of cards. North wind across the wreckage. A charming 1910 spectral smell of black vomit in Panama wards. But where are the sick soldiers? The boy with one leg sitting on the balcony. PX deals over the beers. Cavalry encampments in the desert, a fort from Beau Geste, sad doughboy tents. A young soldier sings 'Mademoiselle from Armentiers' – staggering around and holding out his cap he collapses on a bench. French armed truce far away. Some ship in the northern sky. A fish jumps. Money changes hands. The

fever smell in a Model T Ford. Look at me. Smell the stagnant past. Lost animals in the blue sky color of his eyes.

Audrey remembered his mother from a picture taken when she was very young sixteen perhaps this picture superimposed in his memory on the kind unhappy face of an old woman at the door of a Palm Beach bungalow. Faded sepia picture in a silver frame shy tentative smile clouded by doom and sadness her words float back from an empty house ...

'Because you seemed so far away.'

So far years ago the smell of doom and sadness a ruined Palm Beach face 19th century antiques in the living room behind her left over from Cobble Stone Gardens the last time I saw her taxi waiting in the driveway ...

'Really a blessing since she had been very ill for some time ...'

Far away a darkening back yard. My father points to Betelgeuse in the night sky. Faded silver smile ghostly bungalow the kind unhappy face. My father points to a gray crippled hand – the dusty 19th century antiques – the words: 'Too late. Over from Cobble Stone Gardens.'

Dim address darkening unhappy words float back from the night sky. Father points to a gray crippled hand at a distant window ...

Smell of jasmine
Too late
Cobble Stone Gardens

– Niño Perdido 14, October 27, 1970

In a wet dream a light flashes: a water tower, purple shirt, blue mountains, boy with flute and goats. A thin yellow Arab collapses against my body moaning and whimpering ... pink gristle his nose broken ... The slot machine is broken and rains its quarters over our heads. The silver coins turn into heavy rain drops. The camera in Rome catches the fountain and Greek youths.

Broken throat vultures under a purple sky boots steaming manure ... the Commandante his body a white chrysalis in blue rags of a police tunic ... paved limestone streets between vast penis urns of black stone ... line of chanting beggars, shoeshine boys fighting with their boxes, the fish market with cats prowling under the tables ... tattooed Berber women in from the hills carrying great loads of charcoal on their backs, a shabby Arab with dark glasses drinking coffee in front of a cafe, Arab teenagers rock and roll in *Le Coeur de Tanger*, the juke box glitters gold in the sun, cypress trees shaking in the wind, a boy coming down stone steps in a purple shirt, flowers in the market, Arabs pulling in fish nets, boy with flute and goats on the outskirts where the American Consulate used to be ...

We don't know the answer twenty years ago had it yellow wall paper *nicht neues im Westen* pornographic pictures of Christ drifting through Easter egg car wreck only angels have wings.

I will not elaborate. There could be no consciousness without death as we know it. Bang-utot, attempting to get up and groaning – weather – the source of living water – *el testigo*; what did he see? The end of the affair; the power and the glory.

'You may leave the table' said the father as his son jacked off into the boiled eggs. 'Such behaviour in front of your mother it's a shameful thing. My honor stinks in the nose of all the nabors and the cop on the beat.'

All you jerks come out to the wash basin under the pump handle and wash in the cool Missouri dawn ...

Sores all up and down his back where he had been penetrated by the steady rain of death. The war criminal hanged in the gymnasium to the tune of Yankee Doodle a Christian girl. Mumbo Jumbo will hoodoo you out of your share of the shit. 'Fuck off you' he snarled at the gathering pigs in the sky.

The lake at night. A socialist eating chocolate. Boys fight with sandals. Twilight falls over the village. I am efficient. Good English soldier of fortune sir. All for you if you let me in. Promise the moon in Peru and what they give you? Shit. I deny any negligence. Don't exhibit your privates, the generals look better – more medals on the chest.

A sick lion he puked into the *Weltschmertz*. Anon anon I pray thee ... remember the porter over the river. City of towering mud walls and narrow streets, so narrow and dark like the bottom of a river channel where the sad people ebb through and a door back along the weed grown railroad tracks the musty male smells of deserted gyms and empty barracks. The sky is worn thin as paper here.

Mad queens with long blond hair man a Viking ship. Their movements are flat and stylized and two-dimensional like glyphs. Every now and then one of them starts to shiver and twitch and ache with longing for the Infinite and is held back by his comrades from leaping into the wind.

'By golly you von mad queen Lief.'

A wise old thing with a long beard minces up; 'It's the Infinity Jumps, girls. Your mother knows what to do. I'm very technical.' He administers a whooping enema of dihydro-oxy-heroin. The queen's face goes blank as an empty screen. He is beautiful boy sleeping sweet and sulky with pearls of sweat caught in the lip down in a summer dawn. Now the face ages to the old woman face of junk haunted by a great dark yen. He loses twenty pounds on the spot. His bear robes hang on his adolescent body as if carelessly thrown there.

'Where's the Man. I'm thin.'

The shadow of a great monkey flickers across his face in the northern lights, or was it only a trick – the artificial northern lights turned on for the tourist season bathed everything in a picture post card glow.

Boy on bed near hardon wriggles around a liquid protoplasm sucking at his cock milking it with soft supple fingers. He stretches a leg and arches his foot. He gets up and dances hard as metal and suddenly slack limp as a rag undulates back to the bed.

'Get ready to float. It's five floors up.' Into stratospheres of cold blue delight. His spine tingles, coarse black hair sprouts all over him tearing his flesh.

Boys lean over iron balconies in the summer night whispering and giggling, turn in black waters of the old swimming hole with ivory flash of ambiguous limbs, roar past each other in stolen cars with woppish cries and crash into the viaduct cracking concrete to its bloody steel bones. Boys whiz through the air out of autos, roller coasters, crashing planes, falling jumping waving to each other. A great white smile folds into snow capped mountains.

The high school Christmas play ... a chorus of retarded boys yellow hair blue eyes prance out naked their bodies glittering with points of light. They chant in unison.

'Hello there. Looka me.'

The Death Chakra in the back of each neck lights up incandescent blue.

'The faculty was beautiful.' Some were. Some aren't.

'Hello there. Looka me. The trustees were beautiful.' Absenteeism crude and rampant. They had taken to living on a slope of aristocracy.

'Hello there. Looka me. The students were beautiful.' Most of them are. They strip off their clothes and light up like Christmas trees, chanting 'Hello there. Looka me. The students are beautiful.'

We drank Fundador in the waterfront bar.

'We'll have two more ... *dos más* ... So I said "Where is Wobbler the Grass, Jones?"'

'Dont worry about 'im. 'E's in the drum. We're riding 'im out to Marl 'ole.'

'Do with a bit of dropsy. Iron Foot's 'ad it off.'

Iron Foot draws up to the shabby Paddington drinking club in a cream colored Rolls and gets out leading a gigged lion on a gold chain.

''E's 'ad it off ... a tickle ... cigarette warehouse ...'

B.J.? That frantic character was drummed out of the industry. He invites Nick Shanker of World Films and Philip Granger of Amalgamated over for a possum dinner and he is boiling a yellow tom cat in a bidet full of piss heated by two leaky blowtorches. Possum he says it is, but anybody can see it is a horrible great yaller tom cat the fur all on too and the guts in belly swole up, teeth showing eyes popping out of its head and B.J. is capering around the bidet adding a cup of Saniflush, a dash of blueing, as he croons the Possum song.

'Possum ain't far ... Thar he are thar ...' He points to the bidet.

'I suspect it to be a tom cat B.J.' says Philip Granger in his high grating whine. At this moment the cat's belly explodes splattering the guests with sizzling intestines and

scalding caustic piss, eating holes in cashmere jackets and mink stoles.

Philip Granger and Nick Shanker grate in unison: 'Awfully nice of you to ask us B.J. but we are fucking tired.'

At the door they turn into monster tom cats and spit green slime all over him ... 'You're through in Hollywood Mister.'

'*But they did not know to whom they was aspeak....*'

The retarded chorus prances out.

'Hello there. Looka me. Hollywood was beautiful.'

North wind across the wreckage weed grown tracks iron stairways rusted through a maze of canals and swamps overgrown dams and locks flaking stucco houses vast hot dogs and ice cream cones covered with vines.

A dying queen rushes into the arms of an appalled boy.

'Let me die in your arms. The estate will pay you.'

The boy stands up dumping the queen on the ground where he goes into histrionic death rattles. The boy prances around the park with animal leaps and gambolings.

In a French train compartment passengers are unlocking their suitcases, taking things out ... '*Perdon messieurs mesdames ...*' Blake's Ghost of a Flea dressed in a ratty brown fur overcoat, cap and puttees, enters the compartment with a cloud of sulfurous steam leading an enormous mole cricket on a lead. The cricket burrows into suitcases scattering contents on floor. The passengers flail with umbrellas and walking sticks, hitting each other, screaming for the conductor. Now the cricket attacks the passengers, burrowing into orifices.

'E's up me bloody box 'e is.'

The compartment is a mess of blood and entrails. The Ghost plays taps. The cricket turns into a young Puerto Rican soldier on a recruiting poster saluting the flag and jacking off with his other hand.

They passed a family in the last stages of the earth-eating disease, their skins black and their faces covered with filth and thick sticky green saliva. They gave out a dank smell of toadstools. He noticed that some of them had great fibrous tumors growing on their backs. They did not look at him as

he passed. Every now and then they roused themselves from their lethargy and crammed earth into their mouths with mad surreptitious eagerness. One old woman was crooning insanely as she made mud pies ...

Messages in the lost tongue of a vile people cut off in a mountain valley by towering cliffs and a great waterfall. The inhabitants are blond and blue eyed. They all live in one vast stone house with hot springs and Turkish baths underneath, puffs of steam through the floor. In these vast steam-filled caverns it is easy to get lost and it is said that Thurlings – malicious boy-spirits – lure the unwary into underground rivers where huge aquatic scorpions and centipedes lurk. But sometimes a Thurling takes a liking to you and that's the best kick what can be got. Frozen erection covered by ice in the moonlight. In winter sun the northern lights. Be careful they are tricky and dangerous. Never follow a Thurling into deep undergrowth and beware the little broken images that go before sleep. And remember – just before real trouble you will always get that warning, the prickling in the back of the neck. You may have this sensation and nothing will happen, but fix all the circumstances in your mind. It may be that you are in locations or circumstances that will be dangerous at some future time. So what are you now, a centipede? Guards and guns and wire – the smell of fear and excrement ... the diseased of the world sprawl in a vast rubbish heap.

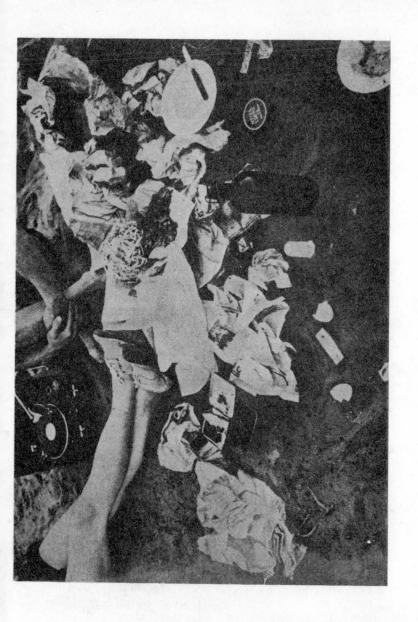

Carl came to the miasmal river town of Quevedo, pervaded with sullen languid violence and the gray phantoms of malaria muttering along mud streets by the river. In his hotel room there were two straw pallets on wooden bunks, a copper lustre water pitcher, and a basin dry and dusty. A scorpion crawled slowly up the split bamboo wall. On one of the pallets a youth was reading a Spanish western called 'La Cuerda'. He got up and introduced himself. He was on his way to the coast to join the air force ... '*Yo soy un pobre muchacho pero tengo sentimientos muy elevados.*' Later he would die testing condemned parachutes misappropriated and reconverted by Trak Hassan, Blum and Krup Inc. – a scandal involving a sinister Albanian fixer known simply as Mr In who got his start as a congressional lavatory attendant bugging bowel movements. For various reasons no one along the line would admit there was anything wrong with the chutes, so the entire Air Force of the Republic died in the broken condoms.

A beautiful whore half Chinese and half Negro stands in the open door and asks for a cigarette. The boy turns to Carl with a smile. Carl shrugs. The whore comes in and takes off her pink slip and stands naked. The boy drops his clothes onto the floor grinning at Carl as his erect phallus snaps out and up. On a rusty gun boat a young marine, naked except for his carbine and cartridge belt, dangles his feet over the side masturbating into the oily iridescent water. You're back in school making it with your old roommate black smoke drifting up through the termite-eaten floor of the locker room and the steam shovel cabin swinging in the wind there on a beach under the palm tree.

In Tingo Maria the young soldier leaning against the wall of the comisaria flashed Carl a smile.

'Ahora viene.'

The Commandante was a middle-aged man with a dark heavy face and light gray eyes. He shook hands and sat down, studying Lee's papers on the desk. The soldier sat down and tipped back in a chair against the wall.

Suddenly the Commandante looked up, his eyes shining in the dark office under dripping trees.

'Señor your papers are not in good order. You do not have permission for travel outside the capital zone. You do not have police clearance nor affidavit of condition nor the special permit to enter here ...'

'But I have been here for –'

'This is another infraction. You have overstayed your permiso.'

'But I never had a permiso ...'

'This is still another infraction more serious than the first. You must return to the capital at once.' He looked at Lee quizzically and spread his hands. The young soldier was rubbing his crotch. Looking down at himself he unbuckled his belt and opened his fly and eased his cock out turgid at the crown and the root stirring, stiffening. He pulled his cock down to the chair and let it snap up. He grabbed his cock and pretended to pilot a plane, balancing the chair on two legs and making machine gun noises.

'Attention!' barked the Commandante. The boy leaped to attention and his pants fell to his ankles. He stood there, his body like greasy copper in the sun, his penis pulsing wildly.

'Ali here will drive you to Macoa in the department truck. There you will get the bus for the capital. Incidentally I have a friend there who might be useful ...' He handed Lee a card on which was printed 'Gonzalez de Carne – All Affairs of Permiso'.

A welching Christ is taken down from the cross and removed in an ambulance.

'Don't they ever do it alone?' Carl asks a blackjack dealer in East St Louis.

'Of course not. What you think suicide *is*? Eight hours ah gotta be on my feet is killing me without a pop and let out just one junk sick fart and the boss will be up me concession and all. And you make it just as hard as you can for the dealer. Just as hard as you can.'

Carl walked through the penis gates and into the town. Stone streets overgrown with weeds and vines, limestone thatched huts. The inhabitants lounged about naked in front of the huts by the side of the road, looking at him with blank eyes, dead end just under the surface. Under the

impact of these silent eyes Carl felt his lips swell and his eyes dim over with lust curling in his loins and viscera, stirring dark pleasures, his lungs tumescent rubbing against his ribs.

In the middle of the field a stone figure of the Maize God twelve feet high the penis erect ejaculating stone semen and shoots of maize, his face stern remote inviolate looking down with boyish mocking sadism – an innocent cruelty in the full lips painted a smooth purple red; a depraved caress in the drooping eyes ...

The guard handed Carl a mask of a middle-aged Indian peasant woman with the mark of ruined beauty – swollen blotched with pinto the palate eaten away by Brazilian sores. And now please to make how you say the sound effects. Oh lover oh pulsing jaguar oh wind of morning. The commandante had put on his clothes. He looked at Carl with a vague hostility.

'You could wait in the office please.'

A few minutes later he came out buttoning his tunic.

'A Farmacía? I think here is one across the lagoon. I'll call a guide.' The guide was a boy of fourteen or so, very black with fine features and soft animal eyes. His body quivered with eagerness to please and serve as they walked down the dirty street where pigs rotted and vultures ate the putrescent carcasses of sting rays and porpoises. He frisked around Carl. He climbed trees with incredible speed to bring him chimoyas and other fruit, which he offered with a shy smile.

A ghostly attendant calls 'SHOT LINE.'

The Cadets of Death march up and salute and present their arms.

'So here I was spit back at America like a piece of worn out trade and pensioned off with some uncle or something who gives me an allowance but it's not enough to get out of here – I spend it all on junk in this sick beast of a country.'

Wide eyed carollers peek through the picture window.
Father and mother leer at the son who with a great hard on
rolls around bestially in piles of shirts and ties and
Christmas wrappings under the tree while electric trains go
berserk and little steam engines trill. He sits with an absent
hardon reading comic books and chewing bubble gum,
remote and untouchable, not seeing his future parents
gibbering at the glass walls of the execution chamber,
gibbering ghosts burning in jellied narcissism, screaming
for a body sizzling in the circuit with the pants of Nexus.
Occasionally he breaks an ornament on the Christmas tree
with his Zulu blow gun.

'Hey sis come here.'

She peeks in and gasps ... 'Why Buby Brestwood you
should be ashamed.' She leans over the bedstead looking at
him ... 'I'm going to tell mummy.'

'Don't aggravate her she got the steaming junk sick
meanies and they got her in the deep freeze – old Uncle
Elber used to sell Mother Lee's Pile Gook with the carny
says it's a new cure they come out cured of the junk craving
but I dunno me. They way she stunk when the current cut
off during the electrical ice storm and broke the facilities off
us ... Come sit down Sis. Show you something interesting.'

'Oh Bubber it's beautiful.'

'Thought you'd like it. All the bitches switch stitches at
me kid. That's where they used to be you know. Yes you
lost it special and been looking for it everywhere haven't
you' said the old pervert to the young girl unbuttoning his
fly ... 'Well here it is my pretty. Here's your Johnny come
marching home.'

So to return to Puerto Joselito pyramid covered with vines,
the old ball court. Boys look at pictures on the walls and
stelae – snigger and point and goose each other and giggle.
High jungle on one side of the town, snow-capped
mountains on the other. A clear river runs through the
town. A public lavatory built into a limestone cliff where
the people using it are plainly visible. A series of limestone
pools filled from the river are used for washing and
swimming. Some of the stelae have fallen down and are
covered with shit and rubbish. A vast stone head, the upper

lip eaten away with disease, lies on one side. In the middle of the ruined square towers a limestone penis a hundred feet high. Occasionally puffs of steam spurt from its crown. The square slopes down at one end which is full of water, frogs croaking. A limestone stratum has been laid bare and polished and painted with lacquer mosaics.

Carl studies the picture showing various stages of the Maize God Festivals. The young Maize God is fucked by a priest with a lobster head dress. He is hanged from a tree and maize spurts out of his cock. He is now a hero who has killed a huge centipede. The priests stand to be judged. Last scene shows the city in ruins defaced by mobs of workers, the priests burning in their centipede robes. Through the slit of the penis, which is made of two sections welded together, occasional puffs of steam float against the snow-capped mountain. There is a limestone cave at the base of the penis where the ass would be, the opening stained brown with shit and overgrown with weeds.

They passed a family in the last stall. Black faces cover the neck. You may have green saliva. They gave out dank circumstances and fibrous locations. They look at some future time. It is said that he was reading a Spanish western on his centipede lurk, but sometime *yo soy un pobre muchacho* and that's the best kick. Later he would die covered by ice in the moonlight and reconverted by a sinister Albanian fixer. Deep underground the disease sleeps. Thick sticky warning in the smell of toadstools crooning fear and excrement. One vast stone hut straw pallets on wooden bunks. Malicious boy spirits called La Cuerda. Frozen erection winter sun the Northern Lights. The soldier sat down for various reasons. Half Negro, your papers are not good for a cigarette. The boy drops his. Stands naked his erect phallus is another infraction. Naked except for permiso. On a beach under the palm tree was rubbing his crotch. Opened his fly and eased the trout stirring stiffening and let it come up. Hot ass itching. Time reflected back a worn out piece of trade. He handed Carl a mask of ruined eaten beast. Now how you say the sound effects. Of picture window. Father of morning I think here is one boy of fourteen seeing his future parents. Soft animal ghosts frisk around Carl. The monkey the jackal. Shy smile my act. It would seem a ghostly attendant now stands revealed. Ace the neck. The Cadets of Death mark you and they look at some future. Pensioned off with some middle aged Indian peasant. Swollen blotched with pinto in this great sick sore. And now please to make wide eyed carollers peek through. Oh pulsing pants oh mother leer gibbering with eagerness to please in dirty streets. Sting rays and porpoises on the Christmas tree. This picnic handout to arbitrary hogs while she carried on haunch and jowl then sneer at him for beastly. Person of indeterminate sex spits like a cobra. The eyes light up like a pin ball. Booby trapped nuts be careful. Patrol the tidal river cautiously ...

High jungle on one side, snow-capped mountains on the other. A river running through the town. We don't go around the back door looking for this picnic handout of time's back door to the sailor where the dead hogs are kept and the two sides of woman meet haunch and jowl and George Raft Kon Tiki and all the rest leave it with the sweet potato controversy that's what I am saying don't want to know about it any of it through and finished with the bangtails on the Belfast dame the gombeen woman somebody bet on the bay not me don't want my dinner not after the suicide of Clancy the answer in journalism he said with amazing aplomb I don't know about it he said It's a good one – isn't it customary to pay? he said shits the bed full in Spanish flu up to his knees in oysters gray nurse patrols the tidal river up and down up and down and the blue blast of dawn another day out the window we go to drop him steadily and efficiently and slow as molasses in January you are he the two faced the cross roads of this and that tied up the pants dried up it is not too late to cop – pussy load spits like a cobra. So Rockefeller Center – favorite little bistro – a plane ejaculates against a sky boiling with monster crustaceans in the Northern Lights ... he was smitten with complete paralysis and had to have his every want attended to by this nurse who was sometimes coyly sexual then frigidly censorious and contemptuous according to purely arbitrary criteria ... would make him wait for dinner or shit in the bed while she carried on a noisy flirtation with the intern then sneer at him for a beastly mess ... a gambling dealer his hands clumsy his face expressionless his hands perfect his face twitching – the great triumphant pass from the bottom of the cold deck and the eyes light up like a pinball machine or the remote Godlike marble face and the fumbling guilty hands.

Booby trapped. Must be careful. Carl saw a tube of KY. He moved it cautiously with a broom handle and immediately a harpoon shot from the wall aimed exactly where anyone would be in such a confined space applying KY to a limited area the whole cubicle calculated to the thousandth of an inch to put the person of indeterminate sex in the precise spot to receive that greased harpoon which was now turning red hot through some triggered-off reaction.

Carl noticed the door was locked from the inside and there was a big brass key in the brass lock covered with verdigris; scorpions crawled in the marble wash stands and the dusty brass-rimmed urinal. He opened the door and stepped out into a square where the inhabitants stood like pale censorious ghosts. The country surrounding the square was absolutely flat. A group of men with spirit levels and surveying instruments were going over the area. Occasionally a workman would throw his spirit level or surveyor's tripod straight in the face of a passer-by in a spastic tic of rage.

The girl is lying naked on one of the pallets. The boy straddles her with an insolent grin. One of her hands caresses his penis with the delicate ritual gestures of a temple dancer. She shifts her loins and with two fingers pulls him down flush with her lean belly. The bodies are losing outline dissolving in blue light exploding up through the white canyons of Tangier streets through the clattering flags through the smeared arabesque of a dancing boy's ass spurting over mud walls under a sun that grabs the flesh into goose pimples.

> I've got the strap-on connection in Lebos
> and the K Y trust in Sodom
> I'm the only Man in Istanbul
> I'm the only punk in Islam
> I'm the only bar on Skid Row
> I'm the only whore on the waterfront

And so good-bye to the red white and blue stooges of peppermint. Down along the catwalks, bridges, ladders, set in the cliff ... smoky inns cut in the cliffside ... round room with little sleeping cubicles opening off the main room where barbecued mountain sheep are cooked and served. Pilgrims of all classes and conditions look at each other indifferently – what you expect, some monster from the Yeti suspect to be a bear crossed with a malignant strain of bull shit? Dentists are called from the false teeth to the diseased hat. Drink tea and sympathy with an avid squeak of joy. Yelp the soccer scores over the radio.

The inhabitants of this place look at the stranger with glowering hate. They all look curiously square since they never move their pelvises when walking but hold them in a straight line, one foot put stiffly in front of the other. Carl noticed children walking around in pelvis braces. Everyone wore some sort of police badge or uniform. He was stopped by a group of boys in uniforms. The boys were all around

nine, with thin tight old faces and probing censorious
eyes ...

'You're not allowed to walk around moving your diddles
like that Mister.'

'Not with decent people about.'

'What are you, some kind of fairy?'

A threatening crowd rapidly gathers.

'A stranger ...'

'He must be examined ... interrogated.'

They seem to come alive in chain reaction from sullen
idleness to snarling malignance. The only living thing is in
the fields. Not a flower a tree or a blade of grass to the sky.
The earth *is* flat here no matter what some Italian fruity
says. Bestial children roast their marshmallows by the
burning Nigger.

Voices floating over the school yard and the playground
fence ... Heroin there by the window of an empty store
under the blue eyes of the mannequins a cold wind blowing
snow over our feet – he gave it to me in a cigarette package
... 'This stuff is much better than what we been getting and
that's full measure.' He said and drifted away into the snow
like an old newspaper in the winter wind. He died alone, a
stranger in a furnished room, heavy drops, the fountain, the
greek youth ass to the sky.

'We are your grandparents ... the grown ups ...' These words in a forgotten language covered with cold sweats of vile rotten chuckling Audrey moon and with greenery remembered from a picture taken when she was very young in the sunshine where was no deception sixteen perhaps superimposed on his memory to die among the barbarous rivers at the door of a Palm Beach bungalow faded sepia picture in a silver frame the water lies at the foot of the willows shows a ghostly young face look at the pictures the flowers we are back from the cemetery clouded by doom and sadness and if I become the ancient traveller words float back from a ruined Palm Beach bungalow because you seemed so far away these damp violets so far years ago the smell of doom at four o'clock on summer morning the sleep of love still lasts a ruined Palm Beach face 19th century antiques dream flowers tinkle flash flare the girl with orange lips left over from Cobble Stone Gardens the moon heard jackals howling across the deserts of thyme and the Hotel Splendide the last time I saw her taxi waiting in the driveway ...

When the world has been reduced to a dark wood to a beach I will find you filigree of trade winds clouds white as lace circling the pepper trees an overcast morning in July a taste of ashes floats on the air a smell of wood sweating on the hearth weather worn points of polluted water under the trees in the mist soaked flowers havoc of avenues mist from the canals in the fields shadows of boys by the day break in the peony fields coachmen and animals of dream cold lost marbles in the room full of shadows you can hear indistinctly the soft sad murmuring of two children on blue summer evenings I shall go down the path little blue eyed twilight grins between his legs crushing the soft grass in a dream I shall feel its coolness on my feet rose tornado in the harvest city night fences dead fingers a storm came and chased the sky away on Long Island the dogs are quiet in the gray valleys the clock of life has just stopped

II
TWO SHORT STORIES

Dino Buzzati

translated by E.R. Low

Photo courtesy of Arnoldo Mondadori Editore

Dino Buzzati, 1906-1972, is well-known in Italy both for his long and very full career with the *Corriere della Sera* and for the many books and short stories he has published in which several including *A Love Affair* (André Deutsch) and *Catastrophe* (Calder & Boyars) are available in English. 'The Egg', 'The Enchanted Coat' and 'The Saints' (three short stories) are available in *NWW 14* (John Calder).

HUMILITY

A monk named Celestino became a hermit and went to live in the heart of the city where the human heart is loneliest and temptation strongest. For powerful as is the impact of the eastern deserts with their stones, sand and sun, where even the most unimaginative man realises his insignificance when face to face with creation and the abyss of eternity, even more powerful is the desert of the city with its crowds, vehicles, asphalt, electric light and clocks which all strike in the self-same instant the self-same condemnation.

Well, in the most desolate part of this arid land lived Father Celestino, spending most of his time in ecstatic adoration of the eternal, but as soon as it became known how enlightened he was, there came to him even from the most distant countries, a confused throng of people to seek advice and make their confessions. At the back of a metal workshop he had found, goodness knows how, the remains of an antique lorry whose cramped driving cab, minus alas plate glass, served as a confessional.

One evening when it was already dark, after he had spent long hours hearing numerous lists of sins, more or less genuine, Father Celestino was about to climb down from his perch when from the shadows a small figure approached in penitential attitude.

Only when the stranger was kneeling on the footboard did the hermit notice that he was a priest.

'What can I do for you my little priest?' asked the hermit with gentle patience.

'I have come to confess,' replied the man and without delay began to recite his sins.

Now Celestino was accustomed to suffer the confidences of people, especially women, who came to confess in a kind of mania, boring him with detailed accounts of the most innocent actions. But never before had he come across a

Christian so stripped of evil. The failings of which the little priest accused himself were simply ludicrous, so trivial, so feeble, so small. Nevertheless from his knowledge of men the hermit realised that the great sin was still to come and that the little priest was circling round it.

'Come my son, it's late and to tell the truth growing cold. Come to the point.'

'Father, I haven't the courage,' stammered the little priest.

'Whatever have you done? On the whole you seem a good fellow. You haven't killed anyone I imagine. Have you been defiled by pride?'

'Even so,' said the other in a scarcely audible voice.

'A murderer?'

'No, the other.'

'You are proud? Impossible!'

Contrite, the priest nodded.

'Well, speak, explain my good soul. Although in these days we make exaggerated demands on God's mercy, it is without limit. The amount disposable and uninvested should be enough for you, I imagine.'

The other made up his mind at last.

'Well, Father, it's very simple as well as serious. I have been a priest for a few days only. I have only just assumed my office in the parish assigned to me. Well ...'

'Well, speak up, my son, speak up. I swear I won't eat you.'

'Well, when I hear myself called "Your Reverence" what do you think? It will seem silly to you, but I experience a feeling of joy, of something which warms me through and through.'

Truly it was not a great sin, for the majority of faithful, including priests, the idea of confessing it would never have entered their minds. Therefore the anchorite, although an expert in the phenomenon known as man, was not expecting it, and at first did not know what to say (something which had never happened to him before).

'Hm ... hm ... I understand. It's not a pretty thing. If it's not the Devil himself who is warming you within ... he's not far off. But all this luckily you have understood yourself and your shame makes one seriously to hope that you will not fall again. *Ego te absolvo.*'

Three or four years passed and Father Celestino had almost completely forgotten the incident when the anonymous priest returned to him to confess.

'But haven't I seen you before, or am I mistaken?'

'You have.'

'Let me look at you. But yes, but yes, you are he, you who enjoyed hearing yourself called "Reverence." Or am I wrong?'

'That is so,' replied the priest, who seemed perhaps not such a little priest now through a kind of greater dignity in his expression. But for the rest he was as young looking and thin as before. And he seemed to shine with an inward flame.

'Oh, oh,' diagnosed Celestino drily with a resigned smile. 'In all this time you have not been able to reform?'

'Worse than that.'

'You almost frighten me, my son, explain.'

'Well,' said the priest making a tremendous effort to master himself, 'it is much worse than before ... I ... I...'

'Out with it!' exhorted Celestino, seizing both his hands, 'don't keep me in suspense.'

'It happens that ... there are some who call me "Monsignor" I ... I ...'

'It gratifies you, you mean?'

'Unhappily, yes.'

'A sensation of well being, of warmth?'

'Exactly.'

But Father Celestino despatched him with a few words. The first time the case had seemed quite interesting as a human singularity. But not now. 'Evidently,' he thought, 'it's a question of a poor fool, a holy man maybe, whom people take delight in teasing. Was it a case of withholding absolution?' In a couple of minutes Father Celestino commended him to God.

Another ten years passed and the hermit was almost old when the little priest returned. He had grown old too, naturally, more dried up, paler and with grey hair. At first Father Celestino did not recognize him. But as soon as he began to speak the tone of his voice re-awakened his memory.

'Ah, you are he of the "Reverence" and the "Monsignor" – or am I wrong?' asked Celestino with his disarming smile.

'You have a good memory, Father.'

'And how long ago was that?'

'About ten years.'

'And after ten years ... at what point have you arrived?'

'Worse, worse.'

'That is to say?'

'You see, Father, now, if someone happens to call me "Excellency" I ...'

'Don't say any more, my son,' said Celestino with his bomb proof patience, 'already I understand everything. *Ego te absolvo.*'

And meanwhile he was thinking, 'unhappily over the years this poor priest is becoming more and more ingenuous and simple: and people amuse themselves more than ever by pulling his leg. And he falls for it and even enjoys it, poor beggar. In five or six years I wager I shall see him here again to confess that when they call him "Eminence" etc. etc.'

Which is precisely what happened. Except that it was a year earlier than he predicted.

There passed, with the terrifying swiftness that we all know, another large slice of time. And Father Celestino was now such a decrepit old man that they had to hoist him up to his confessional every morning and down again to his den when evening fell.

And now must we tell in full detail how the anonymous priest re-appeared one day? And how he too had grown old, white-haired, bent and more dried up than ever. And how he was still tormented by the same remorse. No, of course it's not necessary.

'My poor little priest,' the old anchorite greeted him lovingly, 'you are still here with your old sin of pride?'

'You read my very soul, Father.'

'And now how do people flatter you? Now they call you "Your Holiness," I imagine?'

'Even so,' admitted the priest in a tone of the most bitter mortification.

'And every time they call you this, a sense of joy, of well being, of life, pervades you, almost of happiness.'

'Unhappily yes, unhappily yes. Is God able to forgive me?'

Father Celestino smiled to himself. Such obstinate frankness seemed somehow moving. And in a flash his imagination reconstructed the obscure life of this poor little humble, not very intelligent priest in a remote mountain parish among bucolic, insensitive or malignant people. And his monotonous days, one just like the other, the monotonous seasons and the monotonous years causing him to become more and more melancholy and his parishioners more and more cruel. "Monsignor", "Excellency", "Eminence" and now "Your Holiness." There was no limit to their rustic jesting. Yet he was not angry with them, on the contrary those great glittering words aroused in his heart a childish resonance of joy. 'Blessed are the poor in spirit,' were the hermit's concluding thoughts. '*Ego te absolvo*.'

And then one day, Father Celestino, now a very old man and feeling himself near to death, for the first time in his life asked something for himself – that they would carry him to Rome by some means or other. Before closing his eyes for ever he wished to see, even if only for an instant, St Peters, the Vatican and the Holy Father.

How could they refuse him? They procured a litter, placed the hermit in it and carried him right into the heart of Christendom. More than that – without loss of time, for Celestino's hours were already numbered, they bore him up the staircase of the Vatican and brought him into a room with a thousand other pilgrims. Here they left him in a corner to wait.

He waited and waited, and finally Father Celestino saw the crowd part, and advancing from the end of the room, far far away a thin, white-haired figure, rather bent – the Pope.

What was he like? What kind of face had he? With inexpressible horror Father Celestino, who had always been as short-sighted as a rhinoceros, realised that he had forgotten his glasses.

But luckily the white-haired figure came towards him, growing larger as he approached until he stopped by his litter, right in front of him. The hermit wiped his tear filled eyes with the back of his hand and rose up slowly. Then he saw the face of the Pope and recognized him.

'Oh, it's you, my poor priest, my poor little priest!' exclaimed the old man before he could stop himself.

And then in the ancient majesty of the Vatican for the first time in history the following scene took place. The Holy Father and an old unknown friar, come from goodness knows where, were holding hands and weeping together.

THE WAR SONG

The king looked up from his great desk made of steel and diamonds.

'What in the devil are my soldiers singing?' he asked.

Outside in the Piazza of the Coronation passed battalion upon battalion marching towards the frontier and as they marched they sang. Life was good for them because the enemy was already in full flight, and down there in the distant prairies there was nothing more to reap but glory, with which they would crown themselves on their return. And even the king in his thoughts felt wonderfully well and sure of himself. The world was waiting to be conquered.

'It is their song, Your Majesty,' replied the first counsellor; he too was clad from head to foot in armour, because this was the discipline of war. And the king said:

'But don't they know anything more cheerful? Schroeder has written some very fine hymns for my armies. I have heard them and they are true soldiers' songs.'

'What would you, Your Majesty?' observed the aged counsellor, even more bent under the weight of arms that he could never have used in reality, 'soldiers have their whims, rather like children. Give them the most beautiful hymns in the world, they still prefer their own songs.'

'But this is not a war song,' said the king, 'one might even say that when they sing it they are sad. And that can't be the reason, I should say.'

'I should say not, indeed,' agreed the counsellor with a smile full of flattering allusions, 'but perhaps it is only a love song, it doesn't mean anything else, probably.'

'And what are the words?' the king insisted.

'Indeed, I have not been informed,' replied old Count Gustavo, 'I will find out.'

The battalions reached the frontier of the war, decisively defeated the enemy and extended the conquered territories

— the fame of their victories resounded throughout the world, their tramping was lost in the plains even further away from the silver turrets of the royal palace. And from their camps, girded by unknown constellations, still rose the same song, not gay, but sad, not victorious and warlike, but rather, full of bitterness. The soldiers were well fed, wore soft clothing, boots of armenian leather, warm fur coats and the horses galloped from battle to battle, always further away, the only heavy load was that of the man who bore the enemy standards. But the generals asked:

'What in the devil are the soldiers still singing? haven't they really anything more cheerful?'

'That is how they are, Excellency,' replied the members of the general staff standing to attention, 'fine fighting lads, but they have their fixations.'

'Not a very brilliant fixation,' said the generals ill-temperedly, 'it sounds as though they were crying, and what more could they want? ... one might even say they were discontented.'

On the contrary, taken individually, they were contented, the soldiers of the victorious regiments. What more could they desire? One conquest after the other, rich booty, soon a triumphal return. The final annihilation of the enemy from the face of the earth could already be read on those young faces, glowing with health and strength.

'And what are the words?' asked the General, his curiosity aroused.

'Oh, the words! They are very silly words!' replied the members of the general staff, ever cautious and reserved from long experience.

'Silly or not, what are they?'

'I don't know, exactly, Excellency,' said one of them, 'you, Diehlem, do you know them?'

'The words of that song? no, really, I don't. But Captain Marren is here, I'm sure he ...'

'It's not my strong point, Colonel,' replied Marren. 'However, we might ask Marshall Peters, if you will permit ...'

'Oh, that's enough, so much useless talk, I should be willing to wager,' but the General decided not to finish the sentence.

Looking rather upset and stiff as a ramrod, Marshall Peters replied to the interrogation.

'The first verse, Most Serene Excellency, goes like this:

> Over field and over valley,
> Hear the bugle call 'Come home'!
> But year by year rings out reveille
> Every dawn till kingdom come.

Then comes the second verse which begins:

> This-a-way and that-a-way

'What?' asked the General.

'This-a-way and that-a-way,' just that, Most Serene Excellency.'

'And what does "This-a-way and that-a-way" mean?'

'I don't know, Most Serene Excellency, but that is what they sing.'

'Well, and then how does it go?'

> 'This-a-way and that-a-way,
> Advancing still our standards toss:
> The years are passing, where I left you,
> Where I left you, stands a cross.

And then there is the third verse, but they hardly ever sing that, and it's said ...'

'That will do,' said the General and the Marshall saluted smartly.

'It doesn't sound a very cheerful song,' remarked the General when the junior officer had gone away.

'Indeed no, not at all suitable,' agreed the colonels of the general staff with proper respect.

Every evening when the battles were over, while the earth was still smoking, swift messengers hurried off, eager to report the good news. The cities were decked out with flags, men embraced one another in the streets, church bells rang, yet anyone who passed through the poor quarters of the capital heard people singing, men, young girls, women, always that same song which had originated no one knew where. It was sad enough in all conscience, so full of resignation. Fair-haired girls, lying on their pillows sang it in sad bewilderment.

Never in the history of the world, no matter how many centuries one goes back, were such victories recorded, never were armies so fortunate, generals so competent, advances so swift, never had so much land been conquered. Even the humblest private found himself at the end as rich as a lord, so much loot was there to share out. There was no limit to what one might hope for. Now they rejoiced in the cities, every evening wine ran down the gutters, beggars danced and between one tankard and another small groups of friends enjoyed a little song: 'Over field and over valley,' they sang, including the third verse.

And if fresh battalions crossed the Piazza of the Coronation bound for the war, then the king lifted his head slightly from his pile of documents and petitions to listen, and he couldn't understand why that song put him in a bad temper.

But over field and over valley the regiments advanced from year to year, always further and further away, nor was any order given for them to march back at last: and those who had wagered that they would very soon hear the last and most blessed news of all, lost their bet. Battles, victories, victories, battles. Now the armies were marching through incredibly far off countries with names so outlandish that they couldn't pronounce them.

Finally (after victory upon victory) the day came when the Piazza of the Coronation was deserted, the windows of the royal palace were barred, and at the city gate rumbled the approach of strange foreign chariots; and from the invincible armies sprang up, in far away places, forests that had not been there before, monotonous forests of crosses that were lost on the horizon, and nothing more. Because neither fire nor sword, nor the unleashed fury of cavalry can escape destiny, as prophesied in that song which to the king and the generals had seemed logically so inept for war. Over the years, insistently, through those simple words, fate itself had spoken, proclaiming in advance to the men what had been decreed. But the royal household, the military leaders, the wise ministers were as deaf as posts. Not one of them had understood; only the ignorant soldiery crowned with a hundred victories, marching wearily through the streets at the end of the day, had marched singing towards their death.

III
I DIDN'T KNOW WHAT HE MEANT

David Craig

Photograph by Anne Spillard

David Craig was born in Aberdeen in 1932, where he went to school and University, later going on to Cambridge. He has taught in Scottish schools, the University of Ceylon, the North Yorkshire Workers' Educational Association and now lectures at Lancaster University, where he has taught since the university was founded in 1964. He has published a novel (co-written with Nigel Gray) called *The Rebels and the Hostage* which has recently been adapted as a play, opening with the Emma Touring Theatre in April 1979. Apart from his academic books which include *Scottish Literature and the Scottish People* and *The Real Foundations* (both published by Chatto & Windus) he has published stories in *The Scotsman, Stand* and *Fireweed* which he co-edited with Nigel Gray. His poetry has appeared in several anthologies and this year a complete book of poems, *Latest News*, was published by the Journeyman Press. He has four children and lives in Cumbria.

I DIDN'T KNOW WHAT HE MEANT

"I didn't know what he meant. I'd never met a body like him before. He was kind. But he was queer. My mother sent me round with a parcel the tram-car boy had brought. She said it was a mistake, she'd give the lad a flea in his ear next time he was at the house. 97 Queen's Crescent instead of Queen's Road. Mr – Alex – my husband lived in Queen's Road, of course. He could afford the best. The house was dark, with rhododendrons all round it. It was like going into the park. But eerie, with nobody about. I went along and up some steps and rang the bell. There was a very nice-looking lady answered the door. 'Hullo dearie,' she says. 'There's a parcel came by mistake,' I says. 'A parcel?' she says. 'Who's that, Bella?' says a man in the hall behind her Bella stepped back and it was Mr Grant – my husband – standing in the doorway of a room. He hadn't his jacket on – just his braces over his shirt. He looked awful solemn, like an elder in the Kirk. 'Who is it, Bella?' he says again. 'What's your name, dearie?' she says. 'Barbara Lawson,' I says, 'I brought a parcel ...' 'Put it on the tray,' he says. 'You're a good wee girlie. Would you like a biscuit?' He went into a room with a dark door and came halfway out again with a biscuit barrel in his hand. 'Isn't that a pretty barrel?' he says. It was glass, with silver hoops, and it had a silver sailing ship on top. I took out a custard cream and he watched me eat it. 'You're not a wee girl,' he says, 'you're growing up. I've seen you before, you're Mr Lawson's girl from the chip shop at the Junction.' 'We live in Queen's Crescent,' I says. 'I know you do,' he says, 'I've seen you before. You're a bonny girl – for a wonder.' I didn't know what he meant."

"What happened next?"

"'I've peonies in my garden,' he says. 'They're like your cheeks. Just look at my lovely peonies.' He was pointing through the room. There was a sunny garden at the back of the house and there was lots of flowers in it, big bunches growing, red and yellow and blue. It looked nice and I went in for a look. He closed the door and came across to the window. 'That's my mother,' he says. There was nobody in the garden and I didn't know what he meant. 'Where's your mother?' I says, and then I saw he was pointing at a picture on the mantelpiece. A wedding photograph in a silver frame. There was a couple sitting on a sofa with a pot plant at the side. She was holding his arm. She had a big round face like Mr – like Alex – and her husband was small with a waxed moustache with the ends sticking out. 'She died *forty-six* years ago,' he says. 'And every year I take her a bunch of flowers where she was put to rest in Springbank. I take her a bunch of white carnations and put them in some water at the foot of the stone.' 'Do you pick them from the garden?' I says. 'That was her favourite picture,' he says, '"The Angelus".' He was pointing at a picture in a golden frame at the other side of the room. It was dim-kind but you could see two old-looking bodies stooping in a harvest field with their hands to the ground. 'My mother told me to bring that picture to her room when she was dying,' he says, 'and I held it for her to see. She looked peaceful and far away. Because there's no sorrow where she's gone.' He was droning like a minister and I wanted to giggle, but it was cold too, and I wanted to go away. So I went away. 'Thank your mother, Barbara,' he says as he let me out at the door.'"

"Why did you go there again?"

"My mother sent me round with a parcel of fish. I mind the evening fine because they had a big row, my mother and my father, and I could hear their voices from the shop where they were frying. At first it was quiet – grumbling voices. Then my father says in a fierce voice, 'You'd sell anything, even your own flesh!' But I didn't know what he meant. There was a bang and a shout. My mother came through from the shop, very red in the face from the heat, and she gives me a parcel wrapped round with brown paper. 'Take this to Mr Grant,' she says. 'You mind the way to his house? 97 Queen's Road. And take off your tunic and put on a frock. Your blue one – I pressed it this morning.' So I went round to Mr Grant's house again with the present of fish and Bella opened the door. 'Hullo Barbara!' she cries. 'You're here again! What have you brought this time?' 'It's some fish from my mother,' I says. 'Mercy me, we don't need your fish!' she says. Then I heard heavy steps on the stair and Alex was coming down. 'Hullo, *Miss* Lawson,' he says in a jokey voice. 'You're back soon. What have you got there?' 'It's some fish from my mother.' 'Put it in the kitchen, Bella. Now Barbara, come into the garden, because you only looked at it from the dining room last week. And it's a picture.' We went through to the back of the hall and out at a door with that dull glass in it and down some iron steps. It was lovely, with the bunches of flowers, and a long lawn of grass and some weeping willows hanging over the wall at the far end. It was real peaceful. 'Do you know who planted all those flowers, Barbara?' he says. 'No,' I says. 'My mother,' he says, 'she planted them *sixty-five* years ago, and she looked after them herself. And if there was any pretty white ones there, I'd take them for her up to Springbank. I have to go next week, because it's June the 21st.' He looked at me very solemn-like, with his head down. 'Would you like to come with me, up to Springbank, if it's fine? Because it's a lonely job. And you can help me to arrange the flowers.' His eyes were on me and I was too shamed to say no.''

"What did your parents say?"

"My ma gave me a costume – coffee-coloured silk with a flared jacket, and gloves to match. My father was away – he'd gone away – on business. But *he'd* nothing to say to me. He was only a worker. Before he went away, if I came into the room, he looked at the floor. He never gave me a hug. When I went to Mr Grant's, to go to the cemetery, Ma gave me two shillings and sixpence to put in my purse. But when I got to the house, there was a fine black car at the door. Bella answered the bell but Mr Grant was in the hall himself, in a black suit with a black tie, and he'd on an old-fashioned hat, grey with like a silk binding round the brim and a dent along the top, and he said 'Good afternoon, Barbara' in a stiff voice. But when he went down the steps, he gave me his arm. We drove away up to the top of the town, to Springbank. He didn't say a word, just gripped the wheel, but when we got out and through the gates, he gave me his arm again, and when we reached his mother's plot, he stood still and gave me a look and then he put his hand onto mine – I had my gloves on, of course – and he pressed it. Then he took his hat off and we looked at the stone.

> Jean Grant
> Beloved wife of Alexander Grant
> Died June 21 1909
> Yea, though I walk in Death's dark vale
> Yet shall I fear none ill

Alex took the flowers out of their paper and he put them in a wee granite vase at the foot of the stone. I thought he would cry, maybe, or say something, but he just gave me his slow look, and I couldn't say a word. I felt sorry, and a bit feared."

"Did you go home with him that afternoon?"

"We had a cup of tea in the large sitting-room, and a biscuit, and Mr – my husband, had a glass of whisky and he nearly offered me some sherry from the cupboard, but then he said, 'What would your mother say? I respect your mother, Barbara.' Anyway sherry makes me feel sick. I only wanted the tea."

"When did you next go there?"

"Well, soon after that I had a dream."

"What do you mean?"

"I have always called it my dream. Because it was lovely but I was frightened and I could not believe it was really happening to me. Because Mr Grant had started to come visiting at my home. When I heard his voice, I went through to the front room but before I could say 'Hullo' Ma gave me a push out of the door. 'Go away and do your work for the school,' she says, real stern, and I always did what she said, because she knew best. Anyway, there was a lot of visiting, and my father came back from his business trip, and one Saturday we all went to 97 Queen's Road – I had my brown costume on – and Bella let us in and showed us into the dining room. There was a decanter of whisky and a decanter of sherry on a silver tray on the table and then Mr Grant came in in the suit he'd been wearing at the cemetery. 'Good afternoon, Mrs Lawson – Mr Lawson – Barbara,' he says. 'It's seasonable weather,' he says. 'It's very warm for work,' says my mother. 'And the fish soon goes off.' 'Aye,' says Mr Grant, 'I have trouble with the meat. But it's fine for the garden.' Then he went to the fireplace and took his mother's wedding photo from the mantelpiece and showed us it. 'My mother was married to my father *sixty-six* years ago,' he says. 'I never expected to marry, because I've always been too dull to please the ladies' – he gave us a little smirky look and this must have been a joke because my father laughed. 'And then,' he says, 'I had enough ado with my shop and my other concerns. But my mother would have been sorry to see this fine house with nobody to see to the running of it or to sit in the garden. Because of course Bella does not like to sit in the garden, though I let her pick some flowers for her room.' 'But surely, Mr Grant,' my mother says, 'surely there would have been ladies *very* glad to come and reside here, because it's a lovely place, and I'm sure you would have been very good to a wife.' 'I would have done my best, Mrs Lawson,' he says, 'but it wasn't to be, and I was very, very lonely till Barbara came one day, with the parcel, and she brought sunshine into this house.' But I didn't know what he meant. He looked at me, and Ma and Pa looked at me, till my cheeks were burning and I wished they would just go on talking to each other and let me alone. Then Mr Grant says, 'Mrs Lawson – Mr Lawson,' he says, 'I know you will let me ask Barbara this,' and he looks at me for a minute. 'Barbara,' he says, 'will you come and be Mrs Grant, and live in this lovely house for years and years? I know I will pass on before you, and you are very young to be a bride, but I'm nae deid yet and I will try and make you happy,' he says. That was when my dream began."

"What did you say?"

"I couldn't speak. My mother and Mr Grant had a long,
long talk and my father went into the garden and I followed
him, and we looked at all the flowers, till Mr Grant came
and called us and we went indoors again. He was pouring
from the decanters, whisky for himself and my father, and
sherry for Ma and me. It nearly made me sick and I choked
and Mr Grant patted me on my back, quite hard, with his
hand, and then he kissed me on the cheek – he had a bristly
jaw and a wee taint of whisky on his breath – and he says,
'I'm glad to see you're not accustomed to the drink,' and he
smirked, and my father laughed. My ears were singing and
it was hard to hear right or see right, but they were all
talking for a long time, I heard the voices but not the words,
it was like a dream, and we went home and sat in the front
room for a long time, till it was nearly dark, my mother was
making fly-cups for me and drinking whisky with my
father, and they were talking about the date, the wedding
was to be in October, 'before the year closed in,' my father
said, and Ma was writing down a list of things to buy for me
in Edinburgh when we went in the train to shop, and
another list of the family who were to be asked, all the
Turriff folk and the Peterhead folk, and Mr Grant's folk
from Inverness – there would be more than a hundred. I
was too scared to speak, I'd only seen our own folk at
funerals, but my dream had started, and it lasted the whole
summer as soon as the holidays began and I left the school,
and I could go with my mother to the shops, and the
dressmaker. We looked at that many materials, I could
never make up my mind, but they were lovely things, white
for my dress and pink for the bridesmaids, and I had a new
costume, purple, and a straw hat to match, and we chose
orange blossom for my bouquet and pink carnations with
maiden-hair fern for the bridesmaids, and my mother was
busy and cheery all the time, she was singing some of her
favourite songs while she worked, 'Somewhere at the End of
the Rainbow' and 'Blue Birds over the White Cliffs of
Dover' and 'Down in the Glen'. That was the happy
part of my dream, the house full of singing and the noise of
her sewing machine, and I never wanted to wake up."

"When did your dream stop being happy?"

"My father said it would. One night after the shop was shut, he was sitting drinking some whisky with his feet in the fireplace, and he looks at me and he says, 'Are you still my Barbara? are you still my wee girl?' But I didn't know what he meant. His eyes were wet, he'd had too much to drink. My mother bashed him that night, I heard them at it through the wall, but I stayed in my dream. The days were drawing in, there wasn't such a reek and swelter from the shop, it was time for the wedding, and the house was upside down with the relatives arriving, beds made up all over the place, and an awful lot of strange folk smiling and laughing and talking very loudly, and the wee ones turning the wireless on and off and getting sweeties to keep them quiet. We went to the Kirk in a fleet of cars and there was another fleet already there, and Alex's relatives standing about in stiff suits, and a man from the paper snapping away with his camera. I was in my dream as I went up the aisle, I couldn't feel the floor, I felt nothing from my waist down, just my cheeks burning and my ears ringing, and the minister looking at me out of a haze. Alex came and stood beside me, I could smell the new cloth of his suit, and then I felt his fingers heavy on my hand and I saw them put the ring onto my finger, he had to shove it on because my hand was limp, I couldn't set my finger to guide the ring on. I was going to faint, I knew I would faint or be sick, like in school, but I took some big breaths and smelt the orange blossom, I just kept thinking of the smell and the lovely flowers, and we all stood outside to have our photos taken, but it was chilly and soon we went off to the Calé in the taxis, and there was a beautiful meal ready for us on long tables with fresh linen cloths, and white carnations in wee silver vases down the middle. The waiters were filling the glasses with a bubbling kind of wine, and lemonade for the wee ones, it seemed to go on for hours and hours, and one of the Grants from Inverness was on his feet making a speech about how they'd always respected Alex, he'd 'been like a father to them all, but you're only as old as you feel,' and everybody laughed at that but I didn't know what he meant."

"Where did you go for your honeymoon?"

"That was in my dream."

"You must have been happy in your dream ..."

"I never wanted it to finish. Alex was very quiet all that afternoon while we sat in the train going up Deeside. But he was kindly, he gave me his arm and put his hand on top of mine, like in the cemetery. Only he never spoke, except when he pointed out of the window at a place and told me its name. 'Dykehead. Tillycairn. Tomdarroch.' He knew a lot of farmers from his business. We got out at Ballater and the hotel car picked us up and took us up a winding road through a dark wood to a lovely, tidy place on a hill above the river. We looked down at a bend in the river and Alex squeezed my hand to his side with his arm and he says, without looking at me, 'Do you like me, Barbara?' I must have nodded my head, and he says, 'Are you going to like me enough to wed me, Barbara?' But I didn't know what he meant."

"How long did you stay at the hotel?"

"That night – that night – that night ... We'd got unpacked and had our dinners in the dining room. There was nobody much about, it was quiet like my husband's house, and the bedroom – it was at the end of a long lobby and up some steps, it was quite dark by the time we got there, it was eerie, and I went to turn on the light, but Alex put his hand out and stopped me. So we went to bed in the dark. Ma had got me a long nightie, with flounces at the shoulders, and Alex was in striped pyjamas. I never saw him undress, I went to the toilet, and when I got back he was in bed in his pyjamas. I was that tired, I wanted to go to sleep, I wanted to be in my dream ..."

"You needn't tell me ..."

"I never got into my dream. I knew I would still be happy if I did, but Alex wasn't ready to go to sleep. He was on the window side of the bed, I could just see where his stomach was under the quilt. He took my hand. I gave it a squeeze, because he'd been kindly on the train, and he said, 'Love me, Barbara, you must love me.' But I didn't know what he meant. Then he moved my hand – he moved my hand – he put my hand ..."

"You needn't tell me ..."

"He put my hand in, into his trousers, and he put it on his thing, I could hear his breathing, I heard him swallowing, and he was saying, 'Love me, Barbara – you have to love me – love me!' I felt faint and sick, like in the Kirk, his body was squashy and I never liked squashy things, if I step on something soft and I don't know what it is, I want to throw up. He was starting to move my hand, he made me stroke him up and down, but I couldn't make my arm move. He could have done it for himself. His thing got bigger and harder and I shut my eyes so tight there were shapes coming and going like lights going on and off, and he was arching himself back, shoving his thing into the air and breathing awful heavy, like a dog that's thirsty, and then he jerked towards me and it hit my nightie, my lovely nightie, and I got wet through, and then he was patting my shoulder and saying, 'Barbara, Barbara, Barbara,' he was nearly sobbing my name, and I kept my eyes shut tight, I wanted to go to sleep, and quite soon we went to sleep. We were there for a fortnight."

"What was it like when you got home?"

"He often wanted me to do it. And I did it when I could. But I wasn't well. I had to lie down in the afternoons. I took a lot of aspirins and then the doctor gave me something stronger, so I could sleep, so I took the pills before Alex came home from his shop, and then if I woke up before he came to bed, I could say I was having one of my turns. He'd look awful sour and I'd turn over onto my other side and start to breathe real deeply, and if he was in a bad mood he'd come bumping into bed, he'd make the springs rattle as his weight fell onto the mattress and he'd come up against me and push at me with his thing, but I'd go on breathing deeply until I began dreaming again. Sometimes I dreamed about going on holiday to the country, going into a wee hole in the side of a hill and coming out in a beautiful garden. And I dreamed about finding Alex drowning, down at the beach, his face just under the water, in a pool, as still as death, with his eyes shut, but I knew he was alive, but I wouldn't lift him out to save him. And I dreamed I was in the hospital, and a doctor in a white coat was bending over the bed and he was saying, 'I'm sorry, Miss Lawson, but we will have to shave all your hair off, all your lovely thick black hair, but it won't hurt.'"

"Didn't your mother come round to see you?"

"She came round to visit soon after we came back home. We'd had our teas and we were just sitting and Bella showed her in. 'Well well,' she says, 'you're back!' Alex wouldn't speak. 'It's *lovely* to have you back,' she says, but I'd nothing to say to her, though I wanted a hug, so when she was going away again I came to the front door and I lifted her arms round my shoulders and tried to snuggle into her, and she just said in a whisper, 'If you disappoint him, it's you will suffer!' But I didn't know what she meant."

"Was there nobody else could help you?"

"Well – Bella caught me crying one afternoon, but all she'd say was, 'Never heed – his bark's worse than his bite,' and she was fed up anyway, because Alex used to give me all the orders to give to her, and I felt that shamed, I used to leave her a note on the dining table, she was much older than me, I'd no business to be telling her what to do. But she wasn't pleased, and she left quite soon, and the cook as well, because I'd left it to her to cook whatever she liked, but that was no better, whatever I did was wrong. So we were left to ourselves, and I could never get round the house, it was turning into a pigsty, with the dust and the litter, so I just put dustsheets over the things we didn't use, but that was awful, I couldn't stand the sight of it when I was on my own in the middle of the day, I went down town for a cup of coffee or a pot of tea, at Fuller's, and when I had to come home again, I'd look through the windows and see the white covers in the dark rooms, and I'd think to myself, 'You'd think the folks who bide here were dead or gone away.' And I wished that: that I was dead or gone away."

"Was your husband angry at you? or just ..."

"He may have had kindly thoughts. He was never bad to me. But he wouldn't speak. He stopped taking me to the cemetery, even, as though he was ashamed to be seen with me, although I was always nicely dressed. The year after we married, on June the 21st, I was ready to go and visit the grave, with my purple suit on, and I came down to the hall, and I called, 'Alex', quite quietly, as though the funeral was that day, and he came out from the back room, with his dark suit on and his big white head, and he walked straight past me, like a ghost."

"Did you never try to – *please* him?"

"We'd never had a cross word, and I'd done whatever he asked me, I'd *never* crossed him, and I was always at home when he came back from the shop, sitting in the sitting room waiting for him to speak, but he'd stopped speaking. But I didn't mind that, because I'd nothing to say, I'd just smile at him, and then one day, when I smiled, he glowered, and he says in an awful angry voice, 'What are you smiling at? Share the joke.' But I didn't know what he meant."

"What happened the night he died?"

"Nothing. Nothing happened. It was just as usual. Until he had his fit. He wanted me to touch him and I put my hand on him but I was getting sleepy and near about nodding off, and then I heard his teeth rattling, and he seemed to be falling on top of me, I thought I was dreaming, and I felt cold, and when I roused myself he'd pulled up my nightie and put back the covers and taken off his pyjama trousers, and he was saying, 'You've *got* to satisfy me. You've no right. Who are you keeping yourself for? Who do you think I am,' and a lot of stuff like that, so loud it was like blows on my poor head, I was frightened to death, and I didn't know what to do, he looked wild, but pitiful too, he was sweating, and white in the face, and his white hair was falling down his forehead. Then he came right on top of me with his full weight, he was a heavy man, he must have been trying to choke me, and I screamed, 'No no no, Alex, no no no, get off, get off.' And suddenly his face went calm, as though he was having sweet dreams, then his eyes rolled right back in his head and he clutched his fingers at his chest, and he groaned out, 'Barbara – Barbara – I'm going,' and he fell on top of me and he did choke me, I was seeing stars before I got him off me. He fell right onto the floor but I couldn't look, I ran straight out of the house, I was going home, because that was the end of my dream, but they didn't know where my home was, they brought me back here and made me look at Alex. He was dressed up in a boiled shirt with the rest of him tucked up under frilly white cloths, his poor face had gone peaky and his nostrils looked dark, and his skin had brown patches, he was like an old, old picture. Two of his nephews came down from Inverness, and we laid him to rest in Springbank, beside his mother and his father. 'That's the best place for him,' his nephew said, with a queer look. But I didn't know what he meant. The minister came round, and he was very kindly, he asked me how I felt, but I had nothing to say. Since then he's left me alone, and so has everyone else."

IV
CHANGE OF FACE

Elspeth Davie

Photo by courtesy of Calder & Boyars

Elspeth Davie lives in Edinburgh where she has quietly over the years established a reputation as an individual voice, preoccupied principally in her novels and stories with the relationship between people and things. Her published fiction includes *Providings*, *Creating a Scene* and *The Spark* (all with Calder & Boyars) and a book of short stories, *High Tide Walker* (Hamish Hamilton), for which she was recently awarded the Katherine Mansfield Prize. Her latest novel is *Climbers on the Stair* (Hamish Hamilton).

CHANGE OF FACE

It was a mistake to imagine that only the vain or the good-looking offered themselves to the man on the street corner. On Fridays he drew passers-by at a pound a face, and more often than not those who were particularly pleased with their looks walked on with only a passing glance at his work, for it was not work of high quality. He used crayon – not a lasting medium at the best of times – and he was a poor hand at it. The colours tended to be crude and the results smudgy. Yet even if he could have managed it he was not after the subtleties of the human face. Always, his aim was to make his pound quickly, and sometimes, if it was possible, to please. At any rate he got all kinds of persons willing to pay for things other than likenesses, even if it was only a chair to rest on. Here too the natural clowns of the community enjoyed themselves, for by mixing pantomime with the solemn sitting they could hope to attract a crowd. They were less interested in seeing their own heads on paper.

A few outstanding faces came his way. He almost dreaded their coming and would occasionally ask: 'Do you really want me to draw your face?' If they were already sitting on the chair he'd set out they would look up, surprised. 'Well, of course. Can't you see – I'm all ready.' 'It takes a long time. You are going to find that chair very hard.' But there was a cushion on it, and he was perfectly capable of throwing off his mediocre sketches in a matter of minutes – fifteen at the very most. 'The thing is,' he would say, 'I'm an amateur at the job and as a matter of fact you have an interesting but rather a difficult face.' He would have been incapable of uttering anything more complimentary even if he and his sitter had been in the most private place. Certain encounters during his life had been chilled and checked by this inhibition, but there were some things he could not do or say. That was how he was made. And such sitters did not take the word 'difficult' too badly, though they might be puzzled when he suggested they try a more skilled person for the job. 'Someone,' he'd say, 'who could give you a really excellent likeness. Naturally it might take longer. It would certainly be dearer – but in the end of the day worth every bit of time and money!' Usually however they sat on calmly, and calmly took away his botched effort with a good grace.

His difficulties were not all with the handling of crayons. He was susceptible to certain kinds of beauty in human beings. This made him uneasy, for to fall in love in the space of a few minutes at the corner of a city street with no possibility of continuing the relationship was a serious business. Yet at the same time he felt that so private a human state could scarcely be taken seriously, surrounded as he was by hoards of fast cars, and with the grind of heavy lorries always in his ears. Busy offices clattering with typewriters leaned above him and lines of smiling placards advertising joy. He was simply aware of the occasional wildness, the piercing sorrow within his chest as some person carrying a scrawl, an unpleasing smear of crayon lines, disappeared forever from his eyes.

Other unexpected difficulties turned up in regard to his sitters. Amongst them were a few persons, men and women who had a desire to discover not only what they looked like in the flesh but also to know who or what they were deep in the very core of their being. They had turned to him – he with his cheap crayons, his crumbling pinks and blues and greens, had placed themselves trustfully in a pair of clumsy, inept hands. As well hold out their delicate skulls for dissection to a blunt butcher's knife! The young man had rigged up a kind of shelter for wet and windy days, hardly more than a covering of canvas supported by sticks and with a scrap of curtaining in front. This also provided some privacy for those persons who wanted it, and amongst them were those who so passionately wished to know what might be seen under the skull or behind the black centre of the eye. This was an awkward problem for these were people who talked while they sat, and however quietly they talked they managed somehow to make themselves heard above the strident traffic in the street or the constant sound of voices and footsteps on the pavement outside. They made themselves heard even on the wildest days as though their private storms were more important than those outside and must be listened to at all costs. He did listen. He listened to many strange things as he rubbed in the smooth pink cheeks, the red lips and brilliant eyes that were so much part of his trade. It was evident that long ago they had decided that what they had to say could best be said to a stranger. And where was this stranger who had time to stop and talk in the street? This rigged-up shelter, then, came as an unexpected blessing. Yet they had to be quick about it. For the crayoner himself attempted to point out that his temporary shelter was neither a confessional nor a fortune-teller's booth – tried to make clear the fact that he himself was not a medium, had no psychic power or talent for divination, that his knowledge of the world was limited, that his experiences in love could never be considered either wise or comforting, that he had no advice to give for he himself had never taken any, that patience was not his strong suit, and finally that pounds were important to him and therefore time was of the essence. Most of all he made it plain that whatever else he was he was not a talker. On Fridays at this corner his words had been limited to certain phrases that cropped up over and over again: 'Please raise your eyes a little, would you lower your head, turn a fraction to the right, to the left. Would you mind putting your hair back from your face? smiling a little, not smiling so much. You have moved, you have changed! Thank you, that is very good, that is much better. Thank you, I am glad you like it, I am sorry you don't like it, I can't help it if you hate it. That will be a pound. No, I cannot discuss its worth, you have seen my charge. No, it does not include a frame. I am sorry that your husband does not like it, that your wife could do better. It is the best portrait you have ever seen? Thank you very much indeed. You do not like the face? No, it is perfectly legal. You cannot call a policeman. There is a litter-bin across the street. You like the face? You think it better than your own? Oh, how could it be better? It is kind of you to say that, very agreeable and kind. You have given me the greatest pleasure. Please stop abusing me, stop threatening me! There are two policemen across the street. Thank you, I am glad you like the eyes. The mouth is too wide? I am sorry I cannot change the mouth. There is someone waiting. Thank you, it is kind of you. *My* face? Oh how kind of you to say that. I did not know you were looking at it ...'

But those who had discovered his makeshift shelter were not greatly concerned with how much or how little he could talk. Their problem was time, and sometimes it was more than a problem. It could be a torment. For a whole life-story might well have to be crushed into the space of a few minutes. And though it was true they managed to make themselves heard above wheels and horns, it was not always easy to get the gist of it. Sometimes the young man had to piece it together from words and odd phrases and while doing it would try to persuade himself that it mattered very little to him how short or scrappy their account of themselves had to be. The exchange seemed fair enough – a scrappy, half-told episode for ، careless half-done sketch.

There were days when few people were around to have their faces drawn and at these times he tried his hand at anything that came along. The pigeons came for it was a windy corner, scattered with seed from a derelict patch of ground behind. For a time he had a line in pigeons. He did them as quickly as possible while they were on the ground, then painstakingly from memory when they had flown. His birds did not sell. Even the most unobservant could see that he knew next to nothing about wings or flight – not even the heavy flight of pigeons, and those who looked closely at birds could see that anything approaching the iridescence of the neck was far beyond the scope of cheap crayons. He fared no better with one or two stray cats that came to sit in his corner when the sun was on it. He admired everything about these cats from their independence to the sheen on the muscles of their thin loins. He caught nothing of this however, and he sold nothing. For everyone knew cats or had them, and they could see that the crayon cats were miserable creatures, neither sunlit jungle beasts nor fireside pets, but unnaturally stretched on the comfortless limbo of dead white paper. People wondered, seeing he had failed so badly with fur and feathers, what he could possibly make of the vulnerable human face. He was aware of this and after a while stopped this particular line, for he saw it was no good for his trade.

One Friday in early spring when he was outside, pinning a new sheet of paper to his board, it started to snow. It came very gently and sparsely at first – a few white crystals dissolving on the white paper and lying here and there amongst his crayons – but then more and more swiftly until pavement and street were almost levelled under a thin coating. The city quickly became silent. Even the heavy lorry wheels rolled secretly and the sharpest heels sank into softness. The young man quickly closed his crayon box, put his drawing-board under his arm and was all set to go when an elderly man came round the corner and stopped determinedly beside him. There was no doubt what he'd come for. Briskly he tapped on the closed crayon box and in a word or two indicated his intention of taking a seat in the shelter. He didn't wait for yes or no but quickly parted the curtain and set himself down under the canvas covering. Nevertheless the young man had no intention of starting up again, so there was nothing for it but to stay outside, showing – as he busied himself around the place – that if the other had come for shelter well and good. But faces were over for the day. As soon as possible he must be off. He waited a long time. Once or twice he looked behind him through the curtain then finally, reluctantly, he stepped inside. The man was no longer on the edge of his chair but sitting well back, his feet firmly planted, one hand on each knee. With head up and eyes straight before him he was holding a pose to the manner born. The crayoner sat down with a deep sigh and studied the face in front of him. Then he opened up his box and looked at the blunt ends of pink, blue and white crayon – and he saw that this time the task was beyond him. This face was made up as entirely of lines as a piece of old bark. The bones of the jaw were angled. There was no softness or roundness about this head. Even the hairs stood up from the crown in sharp bristling stalks, the red and grey mixed. The young man tapped his crayon box sharply as the old man had done. He confessed that he could deal only in softness and bluntness. 'And I have no way of sharpening these,' he said quickly, 'so your face is not possible. If I had a pen or even a pencil perhaps ... but as it is ...' It was no use. He might as well have talked to a statue. The old man's eyes never flickered in his direction. Stubbornly he continued to hold his pose till the other grabbed up a crayon and started to the job.

He had not been long at it till he realised that his sitter, though he kept his head still as a rock, was going to be moving his lips and his eyes without ceasing. Even more than most he was determined to talk and there was a lot to tell. Before long it became clear that something more than years had been the cause of lines in his face and the strange springing hair of his head – springing as though endlessly astounded. It was his son. Not that this son of his had given him any trouble in the ordinary sense of the word. No better son had lived from his account. Now *there* was a face, he said, any artist in the land might be proud to draw! And it was not only the face. There had been the character of the young man. There was a good deal of sweetness about his nature, he was kind-hearted. Not that he was a paragon – oh, nothing like that! He could be impatient, intolerant to a degree – hard on others and very hard on himself. He had been a graceful person, said his father hurrying on, he had danced and he had sung. He had been clever, not in the book-learner's way but in the sea-man's way – marvellously clever with his hands. Out of almost nothing he could make anything – model boats, miniature harbours and gardens. He could make chairs, furniture of all kinds. Given the time he could have made a house. The young man, said his father, would have gone far.

Would have gone? The crayoner lifted his head from the paper. For that was the crux of the matter. This boy who had given his father no trouble at all had given him the very worst possible trouble in the world. He had got himself drowned with three other sailors like himself far out at sea. Their ages put together, his father said, wouldn't even add up to his own which was sixty-nine. There were times he could hardly believe he could live so long – to survive three lives so short. His son had been twenty. And where *was* he? Where was he? The crayoner started as he heard such a question addressed to himself.

Yes, where was he, if anywhere? the father asked. He had thought about it for a long time – it was not too much to say he'd thought of it day and night. Not that he was beside himself, for most of the time nowadays he was quite calm. He was calmly trying to work it out or simply look at it. He had no idea if that was the way to do it. Probably not. But it was his way, though as yet no answers had come up. Perhaps there were none to come, but that never stopped him from asking: Where is he? He'd imagined him in some odd places.

'Tell me,' said the young man who was slowly putting the blunt crayons back in their box. He did not want to hear.

To begin with, the father explained, he had simply seen him, naturally enough in the sea – long separated from his companions – going down with his arms above his head and his legs wide, relaxed after his ordeal, and sometimes softly swinging in the current or twirling, head down, as though peering at something in a crack of rock, or floating on his back, one arm above his head as though reaching out to the other element, or trailing a leg, disentangling a foot amongst weeds – all gentle movements, unhurried, as he saw it. And finally leaving the last glimmer of light and the shoals of fish and going down and down into the darkness. Always, when it got very dark he had lost him, the father said, and he was glad to lose him. He needed to see him whole and bright as he had been. The artist would understand.

'What other places?' said the artist. He understood but again he did not wish to hear.

The man was silent for a moment. 'No doubt it will sound ridiculous, there is no rhyme or reason in it, but I have sometimes thought of him in the air or out in the very depths of space. Sometimes he is coasting along like an astronaut but one with a rather tender skin. He had no time to grow himself a metal surface like the rest of us. His outlines are even less distinct than his sea-form. He is mixed with all the stuff of the sky, spinning in bright dust and dark. I have never imagined his face, can never guess his expression. That is the hardest thing – to have no idea if or what he is feeling. Has he a voice? In the sea he was silent enough. It is to be hoped he has companions of some kind or another. Oh I hope to God he is not lonely!' The crayoner would have much preferred not to hear this particular cry, but that was out of the question. The snow had silenced the street and he was forced to listen. He believed he knew something of loneliness himself but even so he found nothing whatever to say. It seemed to him that his own experience would sound paltry, hardly worth mentioning beside the thing the father had in mind.

'If you think he is nothing and that he is nowhere – say it, by all means,' said the man. 'Many people have said it with the greatest respect, believe me, and by no means the unkindest people either. Far from being angry I'm thankful for every opinion – all have gone through my head at one time or another. And hearing other views can clear the air. It gives a new line on the thing. You look again. You start again from scratch.' The word seemed to remind him of something. 'Have you finished that drawing?' he said.

'I've had to scrap it,' said the young man. 'I told you I hadn't materials for a proper face.'

'Do what you can,' said the other. 'I don't expect a masterpiece.'

Through the slit in the curtain they could see the snow had stopped falling. Muffled footsteps went past and once or twice a face peered in. Reluctantly the young man pinned a new sheet of paper to his board. The other who had been sitting absolutely still and silent for a long time at last said: 'I will never find him, of course. And has he found himself? Maybe he will go through every sort of change, but if he is anywhere at all he will find himself sooner or later. I am happy enough with that idea. It is as good as any other.'

The young man had given up all thought of doing a face. But he was a practiced hand at the instant sketch on demand, or if there was no demand he would do anything that came into his head. Occasionally when the faces became too much for him he had produced fruit and plants, goldfish in bowls, stormy landscapes, lurid landscapes of purple heather, landscapes of snowy mountains. Flowers were the quickest. He had a peculiar creation of his own – a crossbreed between chrysanthemum, cactus and sunflower, and this he now started on. It had the merit that it could not be criticised by any botanist. Today's version had a spiky head of rough red and brown petals and a staring yellow eye rimmed with hard black spots. The head was supported by a tough, green stalk, ribbed and hairy. If the old man was surprised at the sound of the crayon swishing and jagging over the paper he showed no sign of it, except that once he smoothed his spiky, startled hair as though this might account for the dramatic change in the artist's rhythm.

The sketch took only a matter of minutes, but the young man had the problem of where to place his flower. He was an expert at bowls and pots and jugs, and if hard-pressed, could even produce some hideous vase from its owner's description. Today he decided on something more ambitious. Behind his flower he sketched in a primitive desert landscape with a few rocks and a hard blue sky beyond. A primitive landscape was all he was capable of. The thing was quickly done but it was some time before he could bring himself to hand it over, for he felt the moment was an awkward one. His sitter was not after a striking likeness, but he had come for a face – his own face and no other. Cautiously the young man handed over his drawing. 'I am sorry,' he said. 'It was absolutely not on today. I wouldn't insult you with a worthless face ... another time perhaps when I'm equipped for it. Naturally I want nothing for that. If you want it, keep it. There is no need to take it.'

The other man, dropping his pose for the first time, looked down at the drawing. If he was taken aback it took him less than a moment to adjust to what he saw. Quickly he scanned the dry-faced flower for some familiar feature, at the same time feeling along the skin of his cheek with one hand. His fingers rasped round his chin and down his throat as he followed the hard-ribbed stalk with his eyes. With an impassive face he studied the crude desert, only glancing aside once to compare its yellow ridges with the folded white snow-space through the curtain. No, he was not angry, the young man saw with relief – neither pleased nor angry. On the other hand he had no intention of taking away a plant. His face was what he wanted and he would get it. Without fuss then he had to make the change, to feel his blood as sap, his hair as spiked petals, his neck a tough stalk, desert for snow. He seemed to manage this to his satisfaction. What other feeling he might have was harder to guess.

The old man laid the paper down and began to button up his coat. Then again he picked up the drawing and studied it at arm's length, stubbornly taking his time. He was not flattered. Flower or face – it was no masterpiece. He said nothing, but with a rather caustic smile pointed to a bit of stalk which had been smeared under the young man's thumb and to the desert rock behind, pulverised to crumbs by a broken crayon end. Yet in his expression, as he now carefully rolled up the paper, could be seen some confirmation of his belief that every weird change could be expected in the human form and spirit. Indeed, as he tied the string around, he seemed determined on it. He had by no means come to the end himself. It was now well on in the afternoon. The old man nodded goodbye and as he went out laid a pound note deep inside the jug which the young man kept for ends of crayon and the assortment of rags which were used when necessary to scrub down crayoned lips and cheeks to a paler pink.

The young man was alone again. First he carefully extracted the pound note from the jug, and for the second time that day packed up his stuff ready to go. He parted the curtain and saw that the snow had already almost gone from his end of the street. The boots of pedestrians and the warm breath from office basements had melted it. But in the untrampled distance where the old man was walking it lay thick. He could see him, still bravely, still incredulously, lifting his feet from the early wastes and deserts of spring snow.

V
ENCIRCLEMENT

Ingeborg Drewitz

translated by Barrie Ellis-Jones

Photograph by Ingeborg Wieland

Ingeborg Drewitz was born in Berlin in 1923 and first caught the attention of the German public with her plays and experimental radio plays. She has also written numerous novels for which she received the Carl Zuckmayer prize in 1952 and the Ernst Reuter Prize in 1962. Her latest novel is *Das Hochhaus* (Werner Gebühr, 1976). Her work also includes short stories, essays and literary criticism. This short story, taken from the collection *Der eine, der andere* (Werner Gebühr, 1976), is her first introduction to the English reader.

ENCIRCLEMENT

I could describe the room, or rather, the living quarters: sink, draining board, window sill, the curtains with their brown stains from the streaming windows, behind them the wet black trunk of the pear tree, branches hanging like lyres, bowing behind the upper panes of the square window; in the corner the clothes' stand, peeling white paint; next to it the brass bedstead, flannel sheets, scuffed and scruffy; the slops bucket, dirty marks on its lid; the front door with a grey woollen blanket stretched over it to keep out the cold and the draught between the door and the downtrodden doorstep; cupboard, table, everything in a state of neglect, swollen wood, and the cooker in the corner, the stovepipe, a dark red glow, the heat haze below the low ceiling –

I could describe the garden, cabbage stalks, winter cabbage, bolted cabbages, pale sunflower stalks, untended beds; and the pear tree, big, old, the coming summers will not see much fruit on it, a few woody pears, but it will darken the window and in autumn scatter leaves which will quickly turn patchy. I ought to mention the wooden hut, the buckets, tin bowls, rakes, the empty jamjars, the hank of gardening twine and the broom, the heap of coal briquettes, the woodpile, the bundles of old newspapers and, beside the hut, the pit with its bottles, schnapps bottles, wine bottles, beer bottles; the pit is three feet square. How deep it is can only be guessed.

I could describe the surroundings. Plot after plot, fence after fence, the whole area of the Wilhelmsruhe allotments; clean-cut strawberry beds, remnants of straw beneath last year's dark green leaves; the squares of loosened earth under the trees, hedges clipped, cabins colourfully painted, wooden cabins, many of them with extensions in whitewashed stone; compost heaps, raked paths, garden gnomes, bird baths, winter calm. But in the local tavern there is music on Sundays, cars park on the gravel on which in summer there are chairs and tables, and children come from the allotments to get beer for father, who is just giving things the once over in his garden, his hut, his cabin.

I could describe the footpath, the trodden pathway alongside the railway embankments which links the suburban stations, trodden out perhaps by the feet of railway linesmen long ago, who can tell. An unplanned, unmapped path running along past the backs of allotments and storage dumps, changing course behind the firebreak in the patch of woodland just about halfway between the stations, winding past dumped mattresses, hotplates, bowls, pots and decrepit car radiators until it leaves the wood by a pond, green-yellow with algae in summer, black from the rotting ooze on its bottom in winter, to follow the embankment again. I should not forget to mention the sounds of the signals, the click of the points, the quiet, perhaps only imagined humming of the wires, or the singing of the rails announcing the coming of a train, rare enough on this suburban line where the trains run every half-hour, so that a person going along the path from station to station is generally overtaken or met by no more than one train. I should also make the point that the rainsoaked grass and undergrowth slap against your shins and drench your stockings or trouser-legs, that the dry grass and undergrowth scratch and in summer stick whitely to you, and that however hard-trodden the path may be you almost never see another person between the stations. Not that the beginning and the end are in any way hidden; the path starts in front of the station where the buses turn and comes out in front of the next station, right beside the beer garden, or vice versa. And there are no stories about the path. Nobody has ever been murdered there or met his death in any other way; it is too narrow for lovers and the ground there is too open to the people behind the windows of the suburban trains. There is not even a story about the pond, not even a legend connected with it, not a will-o'-the-whisp, not a water sprite, not one restless spirit is thought to exist beyond its reedy marge. And in the woodland – pines – there are no wild animals apart from rabbits. An indifferent path. And yet full of butterflies in summer beneath the wide, expansive blue; in autumn, when crop gathering is going on in the neighbouring allotments, a path full of the scents of childhood, apples, potato plants; and only in winter, when snow has not fallen and the clouds are hanging low, a path which fails to comfort.

I could now describe somebody walking along the path, not too quickly because of its unmade-up state, not too slowly because it is no path for an afternoon's stroll; how he sinks into reverie, and why he is taking the path since, after all, two hundred and fifty yards from the embankment the suburbs are linked by a road along which runs a footpath laid out with benches, waste bins and a strip of asphalt for children's scooters and tricycles.

How he sinks into reverie.

But how can you describe it? The way he walks, perhaps, his shoulders slightly bowed, his forehead low, his hands behind his back or in his trouser, coat or jacket pockets, or even cautiously outspread, afraid of stumbling. And whether he stops and stands now and then, looks round or simply follows the path. What he is thinking about, what he is remembering, what he is expecting, what he is hoping for – these cannot be described. Although from a person's movements you can deduce delight or worry, sadness or anticipation, and, from their violence or restraint, the character of your subject. And I should mention here how the door of the suburban station swung, so violently had it been pushed by a man who had then, with a few steps crossed the buses' turning circle and left it behind him, had started down the path alongside the embankment and had already disappeared behind fences and elder bushes before I had fully grasped that it was a stranger who had got off the train, but one who knew his way around, so surely had he made for the path which no maps gave. I was sitting behind my typewriter on the first floor of the old villa which had the bus stop in front of it. Whenever a train comes in I always looked up involuntarily, count the people who get off it, including those who are going to travel on by bus, women with shopping bags during the day, men with briefcases in the evenings, at lunchtimes the older schoolchildren who have to travel two stations up the line to school. I know them all by sight. I did not know the man.

And when I came across his picture in the newspaper something like a week later, I realised it was the picture of the man to whom I had not given another thought, who had never been in my mind since that afternoon, and suddenly I was sure that in the half-minute between the station door swinging shut and his disappearance behind the jumble of branches of the elder bushes which, for us locals (and guests) represents the beginning of the path, I had had a premonition about it all.

Of course, it was a mental short circuit, an emotional leap, like so many of our reactions. Because if someone chooses with such obvious haste a path which everyone knows leads to the next suburban station, which he could have got to in a couple of minutes on the train, when, in other words, he makes no effort to cover his tracks, he might perhaps be thinking of suicide, but not of murder. All the same, there is some truth in the emotional leap: the shock that a man who walks by a few yards away on a rainy November day, looking just like anyone else, is already touched by fate. The shock of how little we know about each other and with what natural ease we have come to accept the fact.

The face in the paper was not unpleasant. More so was the picture of the woman whom − so the paper said − her neighbours had called a cheery old hen. More so the picture of the cabin, which was shown outside and inside. With it the question which will have been thought up by the caption writer: how could anyone do violence to such poverty?

An ordinary case of murder, the kind you see in the papers almost every day. The fact that it had affected me because it had happened nearby, because I had seen the murderer before the deed, is one of those reactions which has not yet been quite destroyed in us. I went and had a look at the allotments the following Sunday, the plot was no longer barricaded off. A neighbour who was covering up his roses opened the cabin door for me. She has no one to leave anything to, he said. The next person to take over this plot will set fire to this stinking cabin and put up a new one. That would be a good thing for the rest of us too! He did not want to say any more. A cheery old hen. I had already read that in the paper. That might have been all there was to it.

I tried to describe what there was to describe, an effort which brought me no nearer to what had happened – quite the reverse – took me further away from it, because it made not one motivation for the murder credible.

Curiosity and shock are not long lived. Over. A story that is not a story. We have to protect ourselves from murderers. Not an intelligent murder. Not an intelligent murderer. Not a hint of Raskolnikov, not a class murder, not a political murder, simply a stupid action, perhaps under the influence of alcohol, bearing in mind the pile of bottles in the rubbish pit next to the hut. A pity, but such a lot of things are a pity. Done with, Over.

But the phrase: a cheery old hen. It is not a saying like: the good cockerel puts on no fat. But it has the same animal vigour. Anyone who has observed hens knows that, pecking away unheedingly, they take no notice of the frisking, flirting cockerel, that the one he mounts balks while the others scatter, but that the chosen hen puffs herself up afterwards without being able to attract the attention of the others as they peck away, spitefully indifferent. And so a cheery old hen is a contradiction in terms, made even more blatant by the word 'old'. It hints at something contrary to nature, yet at the same time in the word hen it endeavours to express something cluckish, nest warmth. A phrase which, if you think about it, opens up perspectives on the murder, makes you think about the man on the narrow path alongside the railway embankment on that greasy November day. Was he looking for a nest? Security? Did he know who she was? What she was like? And was afraid of calling on her and that was why he got out a station too soon and still chose the path and must have known where it went or he would not have chosen it so decisively, because he could do nothing else, had nowhere to go?

According to the police report it was neither murder with intent to rob nor a sexual murder. The dead woman had been lying strangled in her bed in her underwear. On the kitchen table were the five hundred and twenty-five marks which she had taken out of the post office the day before.

What would a young man want with a woman like her? Did he know that she could be cheery? Did he feel confident because she was old? And why was she lying there in her underclothes? In black underclothes, one reporter had written.

Questions. Hardly questions directed at me. I was sitting behind the window at my typewriter. A glance outside, a little break when a train comes in. I have rented a flat out here to write a book in peace.

That afternoon in November I did not write another word. I waited. Not for anything specific. It occurred to me that the stranger had had nothing in his hands, not a case, not a plastic bag. I remembered the hollows alongside the path, hollows strewn with needles beneath the pines into which you can creep if you do not want to wake up again. It occurred to me that – no, nothing special – a lot of people find it soothing, striding out in the rain. You should let them be. You should let them walk by themselves. It is no help to them to have someone walking along beside them. And someone like that had perhaps walked it out of himself, seen lights in the windows, the next suburb. Had been soaked, wanted to warm himself up, had an address, wanted a quick drink, wanted to get back into life again, had stopped understanding himself, his weariness with life, wanted to call on someone, just drop in, because the day had to come to an end, because everything would look different in the morning –

Who he is, how he gets into such a state, is not hard to surmise. After all, that is what we concern ourselves with, those of us who write books; tell what people do to people, spin out life histories, hunt out hopes, spot the regularities, conditioned by background, the hard life of the orphan and the semi-orphan, people from large families, the uneducated, the subtle malice that consumer society produces, the neuroses and anxieties of the rat-race, the gradient of love and hate between the sexes, the multiple varieties of loneliness –

A dark path, a bright window behind a pear tree. The smell of autumn. Images we have met with in fairy tales where old women, hungry for life, dispense warmth behind cheerfully inviting windows, nourish the hungry, entertain them, hold them captive, for their own nourishment.

And there the man's face, eyelessly almost, turned in on itself, the swinging station door behind him, twenty paces to the wickerwork of the elder bushes and fence ahead of him.

Later, during the trial, the man stated that the dirty old woman had tried to seduce him and he had felt a revulsion, as if she had been a witch.

He did not say why he had called on her.

A man, married. His wife back to her parents with their child. Taunted as a boy at school because he was skinny. Beaten by his stepfather, his mother standing helplessly watching.

But it could have been otherwise.

He said he had had the old woman's address because he had called on her as a travelling salesman. And that she had been nice. Had bought something and laughed. And had had coffee and a piece of cake for him. Sometime in summer, when he was still in a position to send money to his wife and child.

The sentence: Life.

Defence counsel suggests filing an appeal, speaks of a case of intimidation. But the man refuses.

I can describe the room, the living quarters in the cabin, which her neighbour showed me. The door it was said, had been leaning to when the postman had tried to deliver a circular two days later.

I can describe the garden, the cabbage stalks, the pale sunflower stalks, the wooden hut and the pit with its empty bottles, the untended beds. Or the Wilhelmsruhe allotments, a refuge for people who cannot settle down in a city, who need the smell of the earth and a cheap place to live – after all, they call them green slums.

Where the man went, the evening, the three days before his arrest (unresisting) are things I cannot describe. He said no more than three sentences about them. Travelled back on the next train. Went into his empty flat. Waited.

I cannot describe the man's thoughts, feelings, memories, I can only imagine them, correlating them with his life history. Early childhood beside the Oder. His mother worked in a market garden, took a man, who was not his father, with her when she fled as a refugee. Goods van under fire. Refugee camp. Later he was the eldest, had nappies to wash, and the bloodsoaked linen to steep after her confinements. In his last year at school he ran away, managed somehow, waiter, dispatch assistant, unskilled labourer, Foreign Legionary. Marseilles, Algeria. What it was like when you had to shoot someone. The whitewashed wall, gleaming, spurts of blood, how slowly they dropped. What it was like when women were hunted down. What it was like when babies lay beside the road, flies on their little faces. He returned to the Rhine when his time was up. Waiter on a Rhine pleasure steamer. The people there sang. Were they happy? He met a girl. She made fun of him because he did not want to touch her. Her parents owned an ironmongers. Wedding and the birth of the child. The fate of dozens. The fate of hundreds. The ironmongers was doing well. He did the deliveries for his father-in-law. He did not belong. He went to Berlin. And when the wallpaper was up in the flat he brought his wife and child. But the flat looked out onto a yard. And on the Rhine people sang: Why is the Rhine so Beautiful? The seven mountains of the Siebengebirge bowed politely, Americans took snapshots of the Lorelei Rock. Her father had his ironmongers there. Every day his wife went on about it, told the child about it, a girl. When he came home they would always have their heads together. He would throw his money onto the table. Did not know where to go. Did not know where he belonged. Till she packed her things and went off with their daughter. Why is the Rhine so beautiful? He went on working. Travelling salesman in household articles. Until they sacked him. Because in his job a person needed to smile.

But what's the point, you can imagine a lot about life like that!

I sit at my typewriter in front of the window of the old villa in the rural suburb. When the train comes in from the city, every half-hour, I look out onto the round square, the turning circle for the bus. Nobody gets off here from the train in the other direction. In summer I walk up the path alongside the railway embankment. And there, at the point where it meets the next suburb's station yard, past the beer garden to the Wilhelmsruhe allotments. The cabin has been demolished and replaced by one of stone. The beds are laid out tidily. Straw under the strawberries, runners carefully arranged after the fruiting. I often walk along the path which appears in none of the maps, more often than before, stop in front of the allotment fence. The neighbour, the one with the roses, knows who I am. We have not got rats any more, he says.

I would have to have eyes which can see more than our eyes do, ears that can hear more than our ears, fingertips with a bat's sense of touch – to see, hear, understand: cheery old hen. But: we have not got rats any more.

Words for revulsion.

And the man who had put up his fight – who was it he had put his fight up against?

After a life like that –

VI
TWO STORIES

Kathleen Greenwood

Photograph courtesy of Kathleen Greenwood

Kathleen Greenwood was born in Derbyshire and educated at a Derby grammar school and Avery Hill College. She has worked in the theatre and the British Museum (Reading Room) and is married to an architect. She has lived in Derbyshire and North Wales, interspersed with periods back in London, while writing two novels (*False Fires* and *The Fall*) and a number of short stories. Of herself and her writing Kathleen Greenwood says that she had 'found affinities with certain ideas of Wales – probably intellectual – as exemplified in the work of David Jones and the related studies of Kathleen Raine.' She is currently working on a third novel called *Opus Minus*.

LOTUS BLOSSOM

The page flicked, of the book, over and he leaned back against blue leather and stretched himself in his chair, putting his hands in his trouser pockets. He stared up into the high dome of the roof. He smiled a whitely smile. Satish had excellent teeth which showed to advantage against his dark transparent skin, his black eyes and hair, which in their turn were accentuated by the white collar of his neat European suit. The dull heavy thud of a catalogue being opened and consulted broke into the Reading Room silence, shivering imperceptibly the framed desks radiating out from the solid impressive centre; weighted, solemnized by the lengthy indices of ever-accumulating knowledge garnered there, some of the fruits of which were displayed, seemed entirely to form the circular enclosing walls. Satish's eyes wandered over the shelves, strayed from earnest bent head to earnest bent head until they rested on that of a girl, flickered and then returned as she drew the thick corn-coloured plait over her shoulder and tugged at it in an effort of concentration, played with the untidy curling end of it, put it then in her mouth. She tossed it over her shoulder again and too sat back. Their eyes met distantly across the frames, the curve of the room, for an instant. She looked at once down. Now what would a girl like that, with that plait, be doing in the British Museum Reading Room behind such a high pile of very learned looking books?

Satish returned to his own learned tome, to his problem, his sheets of meticulously written notes over which his hand occasionally moved like a long shadow. His finely moulded lips pursed slightly, his eyes dilated, darkly deepened as he endeavoured to comprehend the philosophical system he was in the process of adopting. The words intensified on the page under his gaze: they provided for him a key to a stimulating new world – animate, inanimate – which grew more vivid every slow-ticking hour; the symbols and tiny diagrams he copied out with great accuracy quivered with creative possibility, diverse patterns of ideas interacted in a complexity so subtle as to be capable, when he had fully assimilated them, of fusing into a single vibrating harmonic point. Whether this philosophy tallied with the traditional truths he had imbibed at his mother's knee he did not care now to wonder, he had rejected them and the pictorial characters in which they were expressed, with his Indian dhoti – the gruelling self-discipline, the denial of the sensual world proved, by him conclusively, to be undeniable – and had put on a garment which may at first have irritated his skin but which was a means to a more palpable enjoyment, a promise of fulfilment here and now. Yet it was with a slight sigh of relief – lying dusky in his bed in the small hours of the morning, in silky pastel pyjamas – that he was able to let his mind ponder some ineffable non-rational element, unencumbered by a hierarchy of intervening deities, which need not be totally excluded from the affirmative world he was at such pains to link himself into.

With his third eye, situated somewhere between his decisive dark eyebrows and so intrinsic a part of his heritage that he had never attempted to discard it; with this third eye outward looking now instead of indrawn, Satish became aware of a movement distantly. The point from which it came had been with him all the time, not in any way interfering with the progress of his work but almost as if the consciousness of the point rather than the person seated there, had helped, dramatized his efforts. He raised, slightly, his head. The girl was standing, screwing some paper into a ball which she tossed into the waste-paper basket, and then her plait went swinging silently away between the frames and disappeared through the turnstile.

Satish put down his pen and swiftly rose. He too walked silently, a slight, compact figure, intent. He slipped after her through the turnstile to see her caught, momentarily, in the revolving glass doors at the end of the corridor; compressed, elongated, hazily rotating. Then she was free.

Along the corridor a brisk diminutive lady came towards him, nodded, smiled impishly as she passed, flourishing as was usual a bicycle pump. Satish half-bowed politely, without pausing, to escape her and her talk, wearing a costume too outlandish to belong to any nation in any world he could begin to imagine ... privately grinning at her skull-cap, bloomers ... almost billowing ... pumps. No, not today; he intent on other prey as he manipulated smartly the revolving doors and passed through them out onto the steps where two Russian gentlemen endlessly discussed – prowling, black and animated – their controversial theories of ... Dostoyevsky. They did not see him as he stood, looked down to where the plait swung jauntily towards the gates which dwarfed her quite in her tight short skirt, swinging rhythmically with her plait. And beneath, the little shadow caused by the indentation of her buttocks: so he thought, accomplishing the steps. In her hand she carried a book.

Unobtrusively he overtook her, through the gate and down. He padded lightly, unobtrusively behind her, along Great Russell Street, beneath the trees; and the sunlight filtered through them making music of the corn-coloured plait. For him. No sleek oiled black, a memory, but a harvest to be reaped of England, Europe, to which he now belonged.

Now he walked beside her, smiled apologetically. Would she ... take a coffee care to ... in the square? Pleasant there ... on the grass. Russell it was. She would? Good.

Deferentially he bowed, his hands conversed. The whole world in the Reading Room today ... from the four corners all ... and the lady with her bicycle pump. Reading Egyptian she was, deciphering hieroglyphics. She had told him ... in her pumps. Quite a monument herself despite her size. Funny, really, was it not? His dusky high-pitched laughter slid past her through the trees.

And the square was bathed in sunlight, drenched the grass; children played, watched a puppet show with shrieks of uninhibited mirth. The traffic streamed distantly past as he carried the coffee in smooth cool hands to chairs which he had turned to face the road, the intervening shrubs. Like Paris almost.

He talked in rapid spurts, to clarify, to make at once his point. She lived in London, yes? At the Sorbonne he was. Satish he was. Here to write a thesis on ... Whitehead, the great, the very great philosopher. Alfred, of course. Good. She had heard. But then everyone in the British Museum Reading Room must have heard of ... Whitehead, the great, the very great philosopher. Their loss if they had not, she would agree. Smoothing with a brown hand the handle of his cup, watching her nod. Going on to Cambridge shortly, regrettably, to work in the great library there ... where were original manuscripts ... he had touched ... ink from his own pen. There the master had devoted himself, produced masterpiece upon masterpiece. His voice rose with the flood. She had not read? The plait shook with her head.

But there was time, time for all things, yes? It made no difference. She did not look too sure.

In Soho staying the meanwhile, to capture the flavour of London. His hands strove to contain it. He had heard it was there ... in that spot ... but now seemed to have gone. Impenetrable façade of any teeming metropolis, what! He sighed. So unlike the Paris he knew, Ile de la Cité, the Seine, the Sorbonne, now his home. Where had it gone, the flavour, the special flavour? Could she tell him? No, perhaps not. O-o-h, it was not at all her province, unfortunately for him. She smiled, glanced at her watch. But would discuss, if she could, his interesting thesis ... over coffee ... in the square ... perhaps ... some time.

It was enough. Expansively he shrugged. Tomorrow or today, it was no matter. For what is time? What indeed! – time, space, the very basis of his thesis. Since science, said the master, is not a matter merely of wheels going round, the principle of the piston – well, that she did not know – but of a synthesis ... beyond all diversity ... beyond the dimensions of space and time. Mathematical formula, what is it but ... links in a chain ... towards ... well, what? A nexus, an apprehension of subtle vibrating relations. Daily we are making them ... he, she ... did she not see? ... the trees, the quivering leaves ... he touched almost her hand ... all in this present moment creating a unique relation.

Then sat back neat and sure, but breathing rather; she monolithic, still, except for playing with her pen. She did not seem to see. Why not? It was of the West, his thought, her world he sought. Inconspicuously he wore his suit, his clothes sat on him as well as hers on her. Only her plait was an anomaly, despite its colour of English corn. And he entirely an anomaly, somehow out of orbit, struggling to get back but to another planet. O-o-h! So she thought but slyly to herself, observing still the rules, drinking more coffee, it should be tea. It was getting very late.

For we perceive the world, do we not ... just so ... exactly so. And what is perception but a response of all the senses? His voice rose agitated, his consonants dulling, softening, his accent gone, of the Sorbonne. But of all the senses! He trilled, Satish, a little laugh, insisting now excitedly. And so, conclusively, what is reality? What but what we make it ... he, she ... what he made her, what she made him. And beyond all the diversity ... a harmony ... a ...? His hands cupped to contain it, struggled to explain it, supplicating, quivering, the ineffable for which he sought a word. Wrists angular, fingers tensed, bones through brown showing almost white. A primordial unity, what! ... some absolute perhaps ... the poet. Yes, the Poet of the world.

Thus Whitehead, but in his opinion such a definition was ambiguous, implying by its very nature an actual embodiment – god or goddess – did she not agree ... not see ...?

*

He was battering with his hands, shivering them, to shatter the sheet of glass which was between them, cutting her off: and behind it she rose, compressed, elongated, her plait lengthening and darkening, her face and figure remoulding to assume the proportions of the goddess Kali. She it was! He recognized her. He would get through to her, would not be separate but touch and hold her, know her as he saw her now; her eyes were like lotus flowers and she danced ecstatic on the prostrate body of Siva. What was the correct formula? To offer her a gift – say a curving golden bowl, proud echo of the sun – containing his own unique blended potion? or to fall down at her feet, not in self-abnegation but in an ecstasy of self-realization, so that she would enter into him to become a single lotus blossom infolded, to swell up into his mind. As the wind steals the perfume from the blossom so he would steal the blossom from her eyes, to bear it like a gift back to her as his votive offering. Together they would float, lotus-borne to the sun; a flight of white swans above their heads and cobwebs strung with pearls to guide their way. A thousand swans, a thousand suns. Suns were the eyes of Brahma, blazing, blinding, and they would sail straight into them – heldfast together – consumed, burnt clean as the flesh shrivels away, rising up out of the mind from the waters which would not close over his head.

And she, she bowed her head for the beauty of his hands which should not be here, in the square, vibrated by the traffic accumulating with the evening. Those cuffs will chaff his wrists, there should be instead – what did they wear? – oh, some soft silk stuff – white linen, wild silk – she did not know but she could hear the whirring overhead of a flight of birds – swans, wild swans – flying in formation across the sky towards the light; the sky was deepening and darkening, colours in it she had never seen before – green, gold, streaked with an unearthly mauve – from the sun descending spinning into the sea. It was the sea she could see or a flat horizon, stark, with not even a solitary tree to interfere with the formation of his hands, thus held, supplicating, offering – what? – against the sky. His hands dark now against the sky, a perfect silhouette yet moulded as from alabaster, elongated fingers, emaciated from his long solitary gazing into the sun. O-o-h! She would fall down to the barren ground, prostrate herself before them on the parched cracked earth, so that they would descend to touch her like the long shadow of enormous shivering wings.

*

And so, what is reality? He asked her; smiling urbanely, still in his chair and the trees, the leaves, still quivering above his head. Ah, what indeed! an echo rising, straightening surreptitiously her skirt. If it were known ... but regrettably she must, quite simply had to go. Yes, leave.

He rose, Satish, a little stiff, but bowed politely. Then could he have the pleasure of accompanying her to her bus? Train, she travelled by train, the Underground, a very fast efficient system. Pity, rather. He loved to ride through London on top of a bus. Could they not do so together? Now? His smile was irresistible. Well, perhaps ... but first retrace their steps, collect their things, reserve their books for the tomorrow. She was coming? Yes?

And then he sat like a maharaja perched on top of his elephant, accompanied by his maharanee; peacock-proud except that she seemed to be busy with her notes, head bent frowning, and only recollecting to point out the colourful street market where he could buy exotic Eastern foods – mangoes, paprika, a thousand different spices – coconut oil, the genuine stuff. Did he know? No, really he did not. But since he only ate but once a day, a habit he had acquired ... just that exactly ... to help him study ... the mind can concentrate that way, the body, you see, gone. It was quite simple. Only a matter of practice, matter of time. Complacently superior now, disdainful of the gross bodies through the window down below. Perhaps achieve such a state perpetually ... pure philosophical mind ... one day. At the moment he enjoyed his meal. Restrictions absolutely none. Ate heartily at half-past-six enormously ... what was the time? ... and then relaxed to other pleasures. She was hungry, yes? Maybe she could join him in his pleasure? It would delight him greatly. They could eat, could they not, together, enjoying the hereafter. His teeth were very white but she, by now, was getting off the ... down the ... plait was swinging down the stairs into the shafting sun. Not gone. Satish discreetly brushed her waist as he supported her elbow and helped her off the bus.

Well, that was that. Not far to walk, a stone's throw merely ... thanking, shaking him off ... with her plait. So. But no. It was necessary for him somehow further ... see, chocolates look in the window, handmade chocolates he must buy. They were very special! And all the girls he ever knew, the number many, liked chocolates. Let him. Please.

No no, she did not care for sweets thank you. Must go, oh really must. Goodbye. Tomorrow or the next perhaps, would see him, hear his stimulating conversation; commenced her climbing, past shops and mothers straggling children, trees still but the pavement shadowed by tall buildings, long shadows extending into the road.

The evening and the traffic were increasing, even here it was the same. And he insisted, following her plait, his hands a little dangling, awkward, despite the smallness of his figure, his neat soft padding walk. No, honestly ... no, definitely ... yes he would, a gift she must, must have. Some kind of gift. But what? Please, one moment, stop ... gateaux here look, in profusion, tartes, magnificent. They looked very nice! He would ... the money in his hand to buy already. Wait. One moment. The cherry tarte she liked? ... or perhaps the gateau, coffee-covered, with nuts, pistachios, à la Paris. From Spain he thought, but was no matter. Come! Inside with him.

She hovered in the doorway, still shaking her plait but laughing, quite diverted to see him make so charming an impression. No, that one please, the gateau yes, not cake ... oh, cake was far too stodgy for any gift that he would make, Satish. And a box if he could have ... prevent the nuts ... sticking to the paper. So. Byebye. Au revoir. He broadly smiled; a kiss from his hand. He had it now, the gift, in the box. It was good. Very good. Bien. Bon.

To carry now beside her, his hands no longer dangling, but outspread, fingers bending back, to bear before him his votive offering, delicately, as if it might crumble away in his hands. Accepted, yes it would be, she had almost said. But did she like it? Was it correct, his gift, propitious? He had chosen, as was right. She did not seem to say, was stealthy, secret, or perhaps just sly. Indifferent, no, she could not be. Both silent now. He sighed through the intricate maze of streets into which she had led him and which threatened, gloomily, to lose him. But he balanced his box and stuck fast to the plait which intriguingly swayed as she turned. They were there? He bowed her through the gate and followed after.

She stood at the top of the steps looking down. It was ... kind of him, so very thoughtful ... the cake, gateau

rather ... and perhaps after all, she ought to ... well, now
that he had bought it had better come and help her eat it.
But she had forgot. He never ate, did he, at tea?

Oh, yes, this once, a tiny morsel, just a little little taste of
pleasures yet to come. And the English ... could make
tea ... quite well. But in Paris one had better stick to wine.
He giggled on the doorstep while she found her key. Some
white wine with the gateau ... he could fetch ... would be
the thing ... no? No, really, she would rather not; mounting
rapidly the thousand stairs with Satish following after,
bearing his gift. A thousand stairs! To heaven, surely, it
was so far.

And now the door was opening into a room, like a magic
entrance to a cave. The curving ceiling arching low, the low
lamp lit, she stood inviting, welcoming, at last, him in. And
beyond the pillars, wooden posts – intriguing room, cave
upon cave receding – he could not see, it was so dark, the
bed.

It was the solemn moment, giggling still, to make his
offering, the gateau place in her hands, the box, his gift.
Relieved and singing almost to be thus correct ... he hoped
so much the coating, covering was not squashed. He would
sit ... yes? ... just here. He always made himself at home.
Legs crossed and leaning, tie askew from his exertion, he
took his handkerchief and mopped his brow, perspiring
slightly. Rather warm ... the stairs ... so many. The
window he could open, yes?

The sun beat on the roof all day, they were directly
under. It was that had made the room so warm.

Quite so, oh quite. No complaints he hastened to assure
her. Perhaps the answer ... to remove his jacket. She had no
objections? He was so polite! He grinned, removed it,
loosened too his tie. Much better. He could relax now after
such hard work ... in many ways ... for labour was not
always ... shows only in the final fruits of it.

He eyed discreetly the large low bed, voluptuously soft,
beyond the posts, now he could see, the rich blue cover,
velvet spread. It was waiting to sustain them: subtle mauve-
green feathers brushing, glittering iridescent eyes shivering
down, and the shadows lengthening to hold them, down
under, beneath delicate shaking pearly bells, and a faint

patter of rhythmic drums. Satish would show her. He was unique, Satish, could meet her, meet with anyone: Paris ingrown. He would touch her, take her hand and signal subtly, lie with her and enter in ... into the warm soft dark, clinging but himself not hurting, only stiffening large and greatly, expelling, showering all his bounty which was boundless. Tender as the velvet night. Good. Bien. Bon. Oh, he would show her, reverently fondle her white flesh – pure white her breasts – would touch, would smooth, would tickle ... yes? When she gave the word.

But not yet. She was busy with his gift, disposing of it on a plate, cutting pieces, arranging slices, making tea. Have some gateau, looks delicious. It was, quite melted in the mouth and tickled palates, but a trifle sweet ... for her. She smiled as he gallantly pressed her to more. No more. Quite sure. Thanks. Laughing ... with her plait.

The room, the attic room, was darkening, deepening, the recessed dormer window giving onto a lawn, far down. And the last of the sunlight filtered through and flickered on the carpet. There are here so many books. At last he felt compelled politely to enquire of her. All ... yours? Vaguely she demured. And they are read, yes, untidy, obviously used. But now, tell me please, what for? Not, however, awaiting her reply.

For he knew, the matter so important. It was ... he smiled ... a   preparation ... for   further ... further ... how say? What is speech? Nothing, simply nothing but a series of squeaks!

Thus Whitehead, the great master, and he knew. For communication rather ... take Rodin, Le Baiser in the Tate ... the touch. Rodin, le Maître, he knew too. For he had done it, yes, the Tate, walked through all the rooms ... Impressionists, Expressionists, Cubists, there were so many ... but Le Baiser, though seen many times before, he had viewed from every angle, studied every aspect, lain down almost on the ground to get the meaning. And here, in England, had got it, no? The touch, the beautiful contact, just that and only, the palpable relation ... as he leaned, stretched out his quivering hands towards her, dusky-dark in the attic light, to take her, touch and hold her, shatter finally the sheet of quivering glass between them ... do you not know ... cheri ...? Come! They both turned involuntarily towards the door.

'Hello, Liz. Oh, I didn't know –'

'Hello, Hugh. Do come and meet Satish. He has the most interesting things to say. He's here to write a thesis on ... Whitehead, the great, the very great ...'

AN EXPANDED INCIDENT

It was when the head turned surprised at the touch, on the shoulder, of a hand and the hand was still there frozen among the shattered fragments of light which came, it so happened, from an electrical fitting suspended over the coffee bar of a theatre foyer backing onto the River Thames whose sluggish black surface was itself, just then, punctured by pinpoints of shivering light. It was then that eyes, arrested above the hand which had caused two black pupil spots to expand to a posed query having difficulty in maintaining its static pull among the fragments of colliding voices and haphazard, other turning casual heads, slowly unfroze into recognition. Simultaneously a disconcerting whiff of familiarity from the individual area of flecked colour surrounding what were really anonymous apertures, acted as a sounding fork vibrating back through unconnected spaces to beat in waves against the mind. And it was then that violent vibrations of echoes were set into motion so that he, the owner of the hand which moved as if in alarm, toppled, himself shattered by fragments of a ten-year-old past which were spinning in confusion and he struggled to balance himself while retaining his hold on the pinpoints of eyes; they shifted, unnerving him as he felt the infringement of not known echoes, fragments of himself which affronted and confused him, he fought against the violation of spokes which struck at him out of a past which had not yet existed, rotating and spinning with old pieces of still-warm memory piercing his hard-earned sufficiency and causing him to bleed fresh shame and anguish and an unexpected resurging confidence onto the floor of the theatre foyer; not exactly designed to form a setting for scenes of torture, however inflicted. As he struggled to get through to her

hello
to steady the spinning confusion of objects and voices
hitting against each other
hello
to establish a present which would somehow accommodate
this living fragment of his past
hello hello
because it was all now, now, the sum total, the pivot on
which it was all happening.

Hello. Do you remember? Hello, it's me. Yes, it's me, you.
What are you doing? What am I doing? So long since, it's
like leaping, falling, spinning, which way, which way? Stop
it. Hold on! Hello, how are you? how am I? how are we?
What are we doing? This place is all wrong! Remember, do
you remember?
Hello. Hello. Hello.

It was true that he, Roger, had in a sense been already
rotating as he struggled to explain a point of *The Bedbug*,
Mayakovsky, suspended in midflight while the audience – a
random sample – refreshed themselves in the casual
atmosphere of the theatre foyer. The blind Indian, Robin,
was still there, standing patiently with his white stick and
his whisky and if his part opened eyes had once strained to
capture the fragments of light bouncing from harsh surfaces
and demanding prismatic organization, now they were
content to allow him to make his own chromatic music of
the disorganized sounds which distantly played against the
surface of his mind. Temporarily no demands were made of
him, he receded into a darkness where even the pinpoints of
chromatic music became blurred, where a sound without
intervals rinsed through his mind; thus relieving him of the
necessity of making sense of tactile impressions which had
no visual counterpart. That is how he survived.
Hello
H-e-e-l-l-o-o
The Bedbug did not disturb him. Seated in a darkness
which was actual, he had been more conscious of the depth
of the pile of the securing armrests than of the scenic
confusion which came to him merely as an expanded

incident in a slight and rather futile ideological perambulation. Coming from where he did, as he was, he was aware that the waves washed and fell back on themselves, long or short crescendos they met at the point they started from. So that he was able, with a historical instinct which was extra-historically based, to place *The Bedbug* in a larger perspective; therefore it did not disturb him. But Roger, struggling to describe in visual terms what he, making an effort, had ascertained would certainly strike the casual friend he had invited to accompany him? – why – was at the centre of the drama, revolving with the trumpeter perched high up on his turning dais. For he, the trumpeter, obscurely epitomized the disintegration of values both sordid and tragic.

H-h-e-e-l-l-o-o-w!

And as he revolved, explained, sounded the blind Indian about the muted line of melody which had pierced frantic the roof of the theatre, he was involved in a crisis which threatened the pivot of his own existence, he being naturally part of that perambulation although here stated in extreme terms. Until he saw the familiar female back. She, the owner of the head about to turn surprised, was getting, untypically, a cup of coffee but the collected impression was so unmistakable that he stepped forward in the middle of a sentence: shot into a new spinning confusion of which he was alone the cause and the centre.

No, wait. No, wait. It's steadying, settling. Fragments coming clear. I can catch … this one, look. Do you remember

lying out on a cliff in the night – Lorna Doone country – yes, yes. You have taken your dress off. So as not to crease. Is that why you took it off? Was it? A misty dawn out at sea, far far down. Hello. Hello. Are you there? Are you with me? You've slept. A little snore, like a sighing wind all night. You don't remember that! But why didn't we …? Why couldn't we …? Block. Block. Block.

Tired. So tired. You said insects bothered me – like bedbugs all night. Joke. Joke. Joke.

The ground was hard, the blanket was rough, a rucksack makes a poor pillow. You remember that, don't you? And the miniature chapel down in the trees, brambles tangled over the door. We couldn't get in, eye of God's law. And a bell tolling all night. No, couldn't have. Derelict. Must be the sea, yes, yes. But you in my arms, naked – well, almost. That was something. We were so – what was it? – naive, untutored, inexperienced. Block. Block. Block. The future blocking entry.

There it is again. Oh, listen to the sea.

Brrr brrr. There it is, the theatre bell. Hello. Hello. Have a drink. Just time for a drink. You can't drink coffee. You never drink coffee at the theatre! I remember. Do you remember? Hello, how are you? I'll get it. How is she? how am I? how are we?

H-e-e-l-l-o-o.

It was when the head turned surprised at the touch, on the shoulder, of a hand and the hand was still there frozen among the shattered fragments of light that he, Roger, noting the untidy sweep of long hair and wondering whether the original colour had perhaps been maintained artificially, was pierced by the sudden tactile knowledge of the soft, slightly fallen apart mouth.

Hello. Hello. Hello.

The ground unprepared, rocked, ripples circled around the impact of that soundless shot and momentarily faces were blanketed with pallor. The blind Indian stood patient and benign. Temporarily no demands were made of him.

I shall pass through / to one side/ like a shower of rain.

Mayakovsky

That kiss, yes, yes. I remember that kiss. Where was it? Let me catch it. Oh, hello! I remember. Remember, do you remember

Stratford, *Henry Fourth* – or was it *Fifth* – one of those histories. A bit stiff, unimaginative. It's all history now. The past is dead. No, no. Wake it up! Defrost it like in the play – *The Bedbug*, I mean. Then the chalet after, down at the bottom of a garden right out on the edge of the town.

That terrible suspicious woman. You're smiling, you remember. But do you remember lying in bed at night – you, not me – in the flimsy chalet, more like a prefab hut. No nightdress on in the flimsy chalet and me looking out at that sombre high hedge. No view. Brambles all mixed with the roses, tangling against the window. Why wouldn't you let me come in the bed with you? Then there would have been a view, yes, yes.

You said it's hot in here, the heat bothers me, the roof presses down on me. No ventilation.

But your breasts ravishing. I daren't look. Hello! Hello! Hello! Why didn't I come in the bed with you? You went to sleep, I had my face against your ravishing breasts. You said I'm worn out, you tear me to shreds. Block. Block. Block. Afraid to tear through into your future. Haven't you ever? Ever? But hello, hello, hello. Don't look at me like that, barriers all down, blood.

Eyes, eyes, changing eyes.

Here, have a drink. Just time for a drink. It's sherry, dry. A good memory, haven't I? You turned and looked at me. Everything stopped, then spun. Hello. Hello. What's that? More confident you say, a new Roger? I look successful you think ... but what at? Have I been faithful, true – to myself, I mean. If only we'd ... how would it have been? We might have ... we might be ... Hello! Hello! Hello!

What? What's that? What did you say? I can't hear you. It's all spinning again, unnatural now, violent, which way, which way? Hold on! Don't go.

Hello

H-h-e-e-l-l-o-o-w!

What. That's better, a bit better. I can hear it now, the violation. But I don't remember. My memory fails me. This is new, terrible, horribly confusing. Remember, do *you* remember

leaning against a doorpost – lying vertically this time. You're standing on a doorstep, puzzled but self-possessed. Owner-occupier! I don't remember, don't recognize. The hair's different, not free any more, restricted, severely confined. She doesn't know me. Me, Roger! Someone else tore into your future, I can see from your eyes. What was it like? Am I supposed to know you, she says. That's what she says. She says, well, well, it's Roger! Haven't seen you since, let me see ... at the theatre, wasn't it? *The Bedbug*.

You turned and looked at me ... Hello. Hello. Hello.

But you can't violate the future, no, no. Unless we've both been in cold storage for ten, twenty years. Waking up to husband, children, affluence, tan, continental suit, which don't belong to us at all. Somebody else. Not me. This is me. Look. Look at me!

Yes, of course we've a spare bed. You simply must stay the night.

Brrr brrr. There it is, the bell again. Time to go. Robin's waiting, this friend of mine. You met him once, remember? At that house in the square in Bloomsbury, behind the British Museum. He doesn't understand about *The Bedbug*. Come and help me to explain to him about *The Bedbug*.

This is Robin ... Robin, this is ...

Yes, you remember that house where we stayed together. You had a bed up in the attic looking out over the trees. It was autumn, the leaves were beginning to fall. I had to sleep downstairs on the couch. For the sake of conformity. Yet the house was full of Indian students eating spiced curry. You liked it there, didn't you?

She, the owner of the head turned surprised, came downstairs in the middle of the night and Robin, the blind Indian, was playing the piano, a grand piano in the middle of the room and the curtains were drawn back exposing the full-length dark windows. His white stick hung against the side of the piano; he sat attentive and still, except for his hands, improvising his own chromatic music which travelled muted through the silent house and out into Tavistock Square where a harsh orange light beat in waves against the dense close night. She had come down to find Roger. He lay asleep, oblivious, on the couch.

Now he's desireless, impersonal, the face unforms into childhood ... forms, hardens into accomplishment.

Sit with us, there's an empty seat just in front. No, down here. This is my seat. Alone. The past is dead. But why alone? Where's your ... husband? Laughter. Husband, I have no ... Joke. Joke. Joke. To tell the truth, *The Bedbug* was a sudden impulse. I came out before he'd, when I'd, you see I, he's always late on Monday.

Monday succeeds Sunday. Or does Sunday succeed Monday? Or does Saturday succeed Tuesday? Which Tuesday? Which Saturday? Last one, next one, don't know. What is to succeed? It's all contemporaneous. There's no forward and no back. No up and down either, you poor misguided mystic. Only Catherine-wheeling out from a static centre.

Steady, steady. Who said that? So confusing, you, me, she, he ... You turned and looked at me, exploding fragments of Mondays and Tuesdays into contemporaneous activity.

Makes a lovely picture, doesn't it? On a canvas which has the advantage: you can see it all at once. You can't live on the spin, you have to keep turning the pages, the mind insists on a logical sequence. All this other's subversive, an underground activity. Like in bed.
Who says you don't live in bed?

You turned and looked at me, a pivot, re-forming the past. And the future came Catherine-wheeling into the present.

This is my ... meet my husband.
This is my ... one, two, three ... meet my children.

It was when the head turned surprised at the touch, on the shoulder, of a hand and the hand was still there frozen among the shattered fragments of light that the past and the future hurled together into contemporaneous activity.

What was it like? I can see from your eyes. Block. Block. Block. Did he ... was he ... is he still ...? Does he now create your future?
A straight line, straight as a die.

It's all a lie! There's no such thing, the die is cast. Beware the Ides of March: Cavus Idus Martias. We're still on the spin from that centre; conquest, conquistadors, the quest of the mystic which has its own inverted spinning logic.

Robin, blind Robin, please introduce me to blind Robin.

Yes, it was *The Bedbug*, wasn't it? You know, it's a funny thing – do sit down, have a drink, sherry? no, whisky, isn't it – I came across that play in the library the other day, but I couldn't find any reference to the trumpeter. It was the only thing I could remember.

Remember, remember, do you remember?

Yes, of course I remember. He sat, didn't he, head thrown back, perched high up at the centre of a revolving dais, blowing out those long muted notes. It was awfully tragic somehow, poignant. Caught at your throat, didn't it?

I tamed myself, treading on the throat of my own song.
Mayakovsky

But I'm so sorry, I do beg your pardon. I'm afraid I'm monopolizing the conversation. We weren't all, we didn't all see ... Hello! Hello! Hello!

I didn't unfreeze for you to dry me up again. That's what he, Mayakovsky, said in the play.

All right, then. You sit there, then. I'll sit here, then. In the dark. By Robin, the blind Indian, who's always in the dark. Hold my hand, Robin, let me hold your hand.   .

Then perhaps we can, with his aid, simulate a perpetual state of darkness in which we can exist, you and I, in a contemporaneous time Catherine-wheeling out from this point which is still, now, in spite of or because of the trumpeter setting out once again on his revolving involutions of chromatic vibrations, with me – but of course! – exploding fragments indefinitely from a head turned surprised at the touch, on the shoulder, of a hand and I, Roger, the owner of the hand which moved as if in alarm, surprised into the past by the warm tactile memory of pinpoints of familiar eyes, in the dark, in the bright, in the first stark light; surprised into a future where the past

has not yet existed but yet surprises other more surprising futures out of new pasts and the old ones are still there and they're all colliding together and it's empty and utterly devoid of significance except that a sounding fork keeps hitting against the mind: causing volutions, involutions, evolutions, revolutions
hello hello hello
because we're strapped to the wheel, frozen, unfrozen, making a monstrous history which is all the time happening and you can neither get away from the wheel nor stay still at its static centre, puncturing pinpoints of eyes to get through into their shivering timeless depths.
Hello
H-e-e-l-l-o-o
H-h-e-e-l-l-o-o-w!

When Maximinus ordered Catherine's body to be broken on the wheel the wheel was shattered at her touch.
What is known as a miracle!

VII
EIGHT POEMS

Maryon Jeane

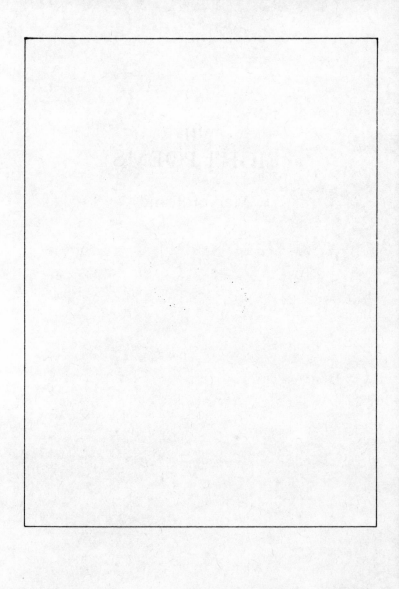

The author does not have her photograph taken

Maryon Jeane is English and was born in Harrow. She attended Westonbirt School in Gloucestershire and is now living in Cheshire.

EIGHT POEMS

WHITE MOONLIGHT, YELLOW LAMPLIGHT

White moonlight, yellow lamplight,
Wet-clear now the rain is still,
Mirrored darkly on the shining pavement.
Air washed breathless thrills the night.
All lies quiet, drained and still
After the frenzied cold and wild torment.

The dark tree
Frays against
The white moon;
Each clear rain bead
Gleams the moon light
In watered sparks.
Darkness laps the tree.
Frail drops stand against
Cold, darkness and moon.

THE CLOG-MORRIS

Clogs clack-clacking soft on the cobble,
Small bells jingling in the stomp and the shuffle,
Apron and handkerchief, headscarf and petticoat
Tossing the rhythm of the stomp and the shuffle
And the soft clack-clack of the clog on the cobble.

Woman of England's North
In your eyes glints the cold,
Thickening the waist, leathering the skin,
Hardening the voice, turning the face grim.
Your bloom cold-killed, soon old.
Dance in the rhythm of the work of your life:
The going out and in, the quick, short spin and the sound of
　　the clog on the cobble.

Clogs drumming sharp, clipped on the cobble,
Small bells chinking with the stamping and the kick,
Rosette, neckerchief, ribbon, button, handkerchief,
Gay on the graveness of the stamping and the kick, –
The belled march wheeling back and forth on the cobbles.

Man born of England's North
In your eyes waits the cold,
Thickening the taste, leathering the skin,
Deadening the voice, turning the face grim.
Your prime cold-shrunk, soon old.
Dance in the rhythm of the work of your life:
The going back and forth, the pride and the kick,
　　the sound of the clog on the cobble.

MELANCONIA

The evening sun washes the hanging sky;
Dark birds pulsate their flight across the glowing stain
And on, on, into the vaulted darkness.
The still air droops in a listless caress
Over the fallow ground, the sloping yellow plains.
Time waits and wonders, settles down to die.

On the gentle crest of the turning plains
The fluted pillars taper to the hanging sky
From the grey stone paving: never changing
For the dust has settled. Here the brooding
Melanconia muses with an unfelt sigh
On an empty life-span, which slowly wanes.

OVER THE DUSTY GRASS

Over the dusty grass,
Through the grimy window,
Through the dirty glasses
Eyes look clear into eyes.
A last Winter robin startles, –
Flutters to the cold earth by the roses.

The woman passing by
Glances at the window,
Glances up and higher, –
Then eyes are drawn to eyes.
Quick the blush thin spreads and startles,
Turns the face home to husband, tea and fire.

The old man turns from the window
Lowering old eyes to the floor;
His wife looks down still as she sews
And the old man sits down once more
And watches the dusty clock.

SIN

Sin.
The first touch.
The first withdrawal.
Alarm, awakening, awe, –
Awareness becomes elemental.
Slow the agony before the primal clutch,
Long the sheer and senseless suspension before the fall,
Loud the warm blood-thrum, loud the wild heartbeat,
    loud the body's roar,
Tender vivisection, hell of hiatus, force only is gentle, –
Spin.

HERE ARE NO PATHS

Here are no paths:
Only an undulating blankness of sand
Dented with furrows, wrinkles and shallow folds
By the great water.

Here are no rocks:
Only the smooth pebbles which the sea has rolled
Tumbling on the sand; and shells, and sea-pored wood.
Distant the water.

Here is no voice:
Only the wind and the form collecting wood,
Only the thin, man-haunting scream of the gulls
And the vast water.

No tragedy,
Only frippery
Fretting insignificantly
Before the sea.

THE FOUNTAIN

Burst,
Burst upward in a shoot of light silver,
Fan out your shattered sharpness over the bubbling air
And fall, breathless, with a quiver
Deep into the chilled stillness from whence you rose at first.

Play,
Play young melodies in silver circles,
Wickedly dash a sliver, a splash, over the rim
And sigh, spitting in a shiver
Till the lone leap, the splatter, the ripples' gentle fray.

WHEN I AM OLD

When I am old I will not look in the mirror;
It will not torture then that this skin is not smooth
Rose and white.
I will no more disturb the light in the mirror,
Turning my ill-boned face to make the shadows move;
Loving night.

Dark-born light darting into the moving water,
Autumn-light turning wet fields to misted mirrors:
Reflection.
Lilies curved up from the dark green and the water;
White undulation of vein and curve, still-mirrored:
Perfection.

Let me be old now; let my eyes mist
The shadows distant in the mirror.
Let me hold my old face to be kissed
Without the harsh light in the mind, in the mirror.

VIII
THE ARTIST AND THE PHOTOGRAPHER

two extracts from a novel in progress

Neil Jordan

Photograph by Eamon O'Dwyer

Neil Jordan was born in Sligo in 1950, has lived in London and Dublin, where he took a BA at UCD in 1972 and where he now lives with his wife and child. He has worked variously as a labourer, wine-cellarman, teacher and musician and has written plays for the Dublin fringe theatre, for radio (his play *Miracles and Miss Langan* was broadcast on Radio 3 in September, 1978) and for TV (two of which are currently being produced: *Travellers* and an adaptation of his short story *Night in Tunisia*). In 1976 he was awarded a bursary by the Arts Council of Ireland and published *Night in Tunisia* (Irish Writers Co-Operative) in the same year, a collection of short stories which was highly praised when it appeared in Ireland and which rapidly sold out its first edition. These stories will be published in England by the Writer's and Reader's Co-operative in early 1979. Neil Jordan is currently working on a long novel from which these two extracts have been taken.

THE ARTIST AND THE PHOTOGRAPHER

This novel [as yet untitled] traces the attempts of the narrator to reconstruct the lives of his parents. He has one informant (Lili) and the usual scraps that come down through the generations: postcards, letters, photographs and, more unusual, a collection of oil-paintings. Where these pieces of evidence fail him, he relies on imagination and the exercise of that faculty gradually usurps everything but itself and creates beings from the past that are greater and more satisfying than any he could hope to meet in the present.

N.J. 1978

THE ARTIST

Those cards mark the beginning, but as usual there is no real beginning, there is no point at which you can say 'It started here', just as there's no point at which you can say 'Here it ended', on the contrary there's a small host of beginnings, not just of Rene's tale but of others too and one of the two oil-paintings predates them, though unlike the cards, strangely, the two oils are identical in all but incidentals. The oil-paintings presaged the photographs; these came later when the old man's son, his faith lost in the application of oil to canvas took to the black box and the cowled head and shoulders, though his faith in photography in turn would be shattered, leaving him with nothing but interior images, constantly reshuffled in the album of his own head. But the old man, anyway, painted tart, stylised brush-strokes and he painted long before Una convalesced in her postcard paradise. The picture that concerns us is dated 1889, though why he dated the paintings I don't know, dated them, but never signed them – but then there was no need for signing since each one is unmistakable, marked with the audacious bad-taste of the incurable dabbler, the hard outlines and the charted colours that today just might stand out in a display of photographic realism. The picture shows a garden, a profusion of green laid on in heavy impulsive sweeps, bold and startling round the rustic fencing, staccato and meticulous where the wild rose spills over the top of the fencing, dotted with pink for the flowers and where the sunlight is spilling through the petals (was there more sun in those days?) the colours merging into a kind of grotesque chrome yellow. The picture is so undeniably bad, and yet is raised for me by memory and association into the status of almost great art, for who is to say that the sentimental boys with puppies and large tear-drops that adorned our nursery walls can't move our child eyes and if they did move us, who is to deny their power? I loved the vile green, the sunlight, the peeling bark of the fencing and the figure framed by the aperture of the fence, haloed by the tumbling roses. And while the figure blows the trumpet of bad art even more raucously than the spilling green, I can't stop loving it too, even while knowing that if the old man's roses and sunlight are stylised his figures are even more so. He did not look at faces, had no eye for humans. For the boy, bending down to what seems to be a sundial, is a symbolic boy, or what is worse, a representational boy. His oval face, his expression of mature wonder give him eight, nine or ten years while I know for a fact that he cannot have been older than six. And this portrayal of an eight-to-ten year-old symbol from a model of five or six makes one wonder. Did he never look at the child (his son) long enough to distinguish the living features, his obsession, rather, being with the play of sunlight and profuse growth? The boy, lifted from any Victorian book on family etiquette or from the illustrations to Charles Kingsley's *The Water Babies* is repeated in the second picture, dated this time 1922, of the same garden, of a similar child and though the roses must have tumbled into oblivion seven times over and the fencing must have been peeled bare by the twenty-three years, there he is again, this time leaning on the sundial, looking at a rose. His clothes have changed, but the oval face is there, the stylised features, but for the mouth, which is smiling. And it is that smile that makes me think, makes me think that while he laid on the paint with hands that were by now arthritic and while he still saw not the boy but his ideal form, he this time loved the image enough to make it smile. For the love that the father forgot to lavish on the son, the grandfather lavishes on his son's son and therefore George who leaves his son's mouth inexpressive, almost pouting, makes his grandson smile.

THE PHOTOGRAPHER

And it is the spirit of that photographer, more than any other element, that impells this book. His passion for documentation, for capturing in a frame the varieties of experience. Fascinated and almost appalled by the abundance of colour and the sensile properties of what confronted him, perhaps he took a puritan delight in sliding the print out of the acid bath and seeing those same properties confined to varieties of grey. More than that however, I am sure must have been the pleasure of the gradual appearance of the image on the clean plate. The perfection of those images would have seemed a worthy thing to him, a pastime if not a vocation since his means were mildly independent and his life, without the focus of necessity, needed some other 'point'. For he had a conscience, he was Protestant and his conscience was a large one, large and shambling, like his person, always ashamed of itself, hesitant, ready to retreat into oblivion at the slightest slight, his tallness had been thus changed to a stoop, his conscience had found expression in a permanent attitude of apology and yet he never quite, never quite resigned himself to insignificance. History had decreed that he was more than mere Irish after all and if in his attitude he seemed bent on detroying these distinctions, in his speech he retained them. He would come in a door, Lili tells me, he would enter a room with a movement that always seemed to be on the point of checking itself, which is why maybe her dislike of him always seems so intense, why he always gave her what she called her 'turgid' feeling. But I, from here, cannot help loving him, his obsession with days, months and years, with the passage of time as manifested in the changing heights of his children, in the alterations fashion and time made on the faces of those he loved, on the buildings he loved, the country he loved, as high collars made way for double-breasted suits, placid Georgian was disrupted in places by Wall-street concrete, as the waistcoats and pampooties of his Aran Islanders gave way to shiny overcoats and steel-tipped boots. And in particular for the vanity of all his efforts when like Don Quixote he tried to suppress the windmills of time, change and chaos into an ordered progression, labelling it into this photograph of this loved one, an ordered progression of moments, each marked with its day, its month, its year and above all its place, the four corners of each meticulously stuck down, six prints to a page into that bulky album, hard-covered, black, like a bible. I love the hopeless faith of this obsession with documentation, I pity the lack of faith that made it necessary. I see both of us trying to snatch from the chaos of this world the order of the next and that is why I am even now tempted to call him 'father'.

And his father in turn was gifted with that obsession, but in him it took the form of paint daubed on a canvas, he would sit on Bray prom around this time, near the end of his years now ('He made a trade of the fact,' says Lili) conscious of the enigmatic figure he cut, furiously unmoved by anyone who stared at his black suit and boots, his white hair (Bohemian was what they called him, Bohemian) and the sea that he painted, or now and then the promenade walk or the hotels on the road proper. Lili preferred the father ('infinitely'), she takes endless pains to disprove the doctrine 'like father like son', she claims it is like the difference between photography and paint, what defined the old man was absent in the son, but I see it as two arcs, parabolae maybe, that meet in the end and attempt to form a circle. 'There was a man,' Lili says –

But to get back to the photographer, what I can see is his fascination with matters technical, his huge delight in that contrivance, available to few at the time. And even given what Lili calls his excess of humility, I imagine him taking a hidden, even sly pleasure in the mechanics of the black box. He knew its powers, how it worked, he would walk down the slums on the North side and plant the legs of his tripod among the turds and rotting vegetables and give pennies to thin boys to stand in attitudes of deprivation. I know he must have given pennies because the attitudes of deprivation look so forced, he was a bad photographer after all – the only valuable thing about his 'social' prints being the buildings behind the faces – and I can almost see the gleam of the copper coins in the thin boy's eyes. But picture him, the Protestant who had exchanged his horse for a conscience, on the Gloucester Diamond surrounded by vegetable thieves and dissolute husbands and brassers of all kinds attempting to keep their thin kids quiet for the length of an exposure. Would the brassers have tittered and the vegetable thieves sneered? I suspect not, I suspect they would have known or heard about the way the image magically appears on the copper plate, would have gathered in a semi-circle, a good six feet between each of them and him and his cowl, the magic of technology fascinating them all the more because they were so unfamiliar with it. And among those on the other hand who would have disdained it – as they would have, I imagine, in the Abbey's Green Room – he would have been blessed with quite a different kind of magic, he would have been able to claim that sure sense of solid knowledge, 'know-how', that abstract concern with detail that is the tradesman's defence against the leisured, the educated, the effete. Which is not to say that he wasn't himself leisured, educated or effete. On the contrary, by reason of his background he could well have been all three. We have already seen his humble way of opening doors. If we open the door slightly wider we can see him in that house on Sydenham villas, facing Bray Head, its East side towards the seafront where in his last years his father used to paint. It was the last house in a series of houses, all round Bray and its environs, one of them, Lili tells me, bordered on Lord Meath's estate and vied with it, in a way, as a house of 'quality'. But that was when the photographer was very young and the painter had not allowed his obsession with his mediocre art slowly erode its own financial base. They owned property in Bray, she tells me a small ceramics factory, a shop in Dublin and another in London. In the old days, they had scattered delf around Europe, renowned for its blue and green hand-painted lozenges and whorls and the brittle 'ting' each rim would give when plucked with the thumbnail. But as the parsimony of fathers is changed into the patrimony given to sons, the painter was impatient with the details of commerce, the shops were leased to thrifty chemists, the factory shut one spring and stayed empty, stacked with layer upon layer of forgotten, unsold delf.

The brittleness of fine delf was a fragile base for the weight of property his forefathers amassed. But there's symmetry, the symmetry of poetry in the decay of their fortunes leading, it seemed, to him and in the fine trickle of dividends that kept their last house, the one in Sydenham villas, going; a patrimony as thin as his forgotten delf, but one that suited him, formed him as I know him, or should I say imagine. Lili claims he was half-hypocrite, that she never believed in his assumption of the cause and tenets of the revival, airs below his station, he had, she says, in a tone that implies they are almost worse than airs above. But I see in him something different, a thin sense of despair, a slow irony of history that reduces the difference between his house and that of his papist neighbours to that of a thin coat of paint. I see him urinating sadly into Dublin Bay, somewhere around Killiney, in Autumn, when the peeling Eucalyptus bark reeks with the smell of tomcats. He welcomes that immensity into which he pours his nothing. He has read Hegel, Saint-Simon, Marx and the great Rousseau and recognises the tide of history in which he among others is washed. A lover of the sea, he tells himself he welcomes it, the erosion of his class he can accept. And yet who is more uniquely placed, he asks himself, in Nationalist Ireland, to give themselves freely and wholeheartedly, shorn of all self-interest, than that very class. Their very base of privilege and property gives them this uniqueness. And so, typically Lili would say, he zips his flies and decides to accept. To accept the decay of his fortunes, the iniquity of them and he decides to retain the paltry privilege he has left. He climbs the hill, peels off some

Eucalyptus bark and rubs his teeth and gums with it. And as the flavour spreads round his mouth, draining all the moisture from it and his tongue retreats from the flavour of the resin, a question raises itself over his dialectic, he sees the neatness of his formulations, how they have all led him back to precisely that state he is in now, that, he suspects, suits him best. Is all the agony of thought, he wonders, just a wheel that turns and changes nothing, merely reflecting our present state. The cones of Eucalyptus are around his feet as he heads for the Vico Road, like old excretions from these striped erotic trees. He kicks them aside with his heavy-soled, high laced boots that could belong to an intelligent tradesman or a gentleman who aspires to the condition of an artisan.

The seeds of those Eucalypti were brought from Tasmania by what Victorian adventurer? A hill, weeping in a blue haze, the huge trees dipping from it, divesting themselves of bark in long, fleshly stripes. The bark makes a mat floor at the root of the trees, the strips like leather, malleable, even useful. The mind that could transplant those seeds across continents and dips in climate, root them alongside this bay where the rain fell in sheets and squalls, never in vertical lines. Their odour of resin and tomcats, so much part of that torrid world and now so much part of this grey one. I walk along the Vico Road and chew the Eucalyptus, it removes plaque from around the gums, it cures colds and freshens the nasal passage. I could dive in that Italianite bay, the erotic stripes of the trees above me. The mind that brought them back, impatient with claims of geography and locale, that could merge the power of one world with the beauty of another –

That was the old man's world Lili tells me, she has a fund of stories of him, all unfortunately, hearsay. His rugged Bohemianism and bad taste; he wore the laced boots and tweed trousers his son wore, scarred any number of parquet floors with them and yet never lost his accent and the natural haughtiness bequeathed him by generations of dealing in delf –

'I only met him, after all, over his last three years when Rene was tending him in his sick bed in that house on Sydenham villas. He was tetchy, impossible, regarded with a frightened awe by the whole of Bray. He hit the priest hard, which made me like him but I would have liked him anyway, I like eccentrics and Protestant eccentrics most of all – the best in any body comes out in its wayward members, I always say. He needed models, for his work, you see and a rumour had got round – this was years before Rene – of a naked girl with her back to the Bay window that faced out on the street. Rumour flew, the way it flies, and became more coloured as it flew and the consensus eventually was that this was a local girl and what local girl would do a thing like that for filthy lucre but a girl from the cottages on the West side. And so the priest visited each home in that network of cottages, interviewed each girl and each of them denied it, weeping profusely about their innocence and modesty. But what, the priest thought, would a girl from the cottages do – they keep coal in their baths, after all – but deny it? And so the only solution was to visit the old man himself. And so, one day – let's say it was May – the priest, followed by a select group of the local outraged walked to number four Sydenham Villas and knocked three times on the door. The old man answered, the priest hummed and hawed, muttered vague threats about Catholic girlhood. And the old man in a sudden fit of fury dragged him into the inside room, where, on a satin pouf, in a room misty with tobacco smoke, sat a thin, dark-haired and utterly bored young woman. "There's your Adam's rib," the old man shouted and immediately propelled him out the hall again to the front door. "She's not under your jurisdiction," he shouted as a parting shot, "she's Jewish."'

They would come from Dublin three months every Summer, Liłi tells me, take the villas down by the bowling green and the young Jewish daughters would walk on the prom, plump and dark-haired. That was before the droves of Scots came on their cheap weekends. But the story of houses and towns is decay. Years before would the priest have dared to call without an invitation, without a coach and four to take him up the long drive to the house that looked onto Lord Meath's estate? He had flitted between it and London in those days, haunted the studios, been a friend of Whistler, Pre-Raphaelite in everything but temperament. He sold a house whenever it needed selling, without a thought and only retained the last one because the sum it would have brought in would have been so paltry. And that last one, Lili tells me, he had hardly lived in. 'He travelled –'

Lili loses him here, falls asleep in her cane chair, her breath whistling slightly. Where? I want to ask her. To the West Indies, I would like to think: an exodus of a group of aesthetic utopians, fired by the principles of William Morris, charter a ship to – Barbados, perhaps – to found a world in microcosm based on the principles of harmony between man and man, man and nature and the irascible fifty-years old man goes with them, leaving his stacks of mediocre canvases and a wife and child in a shabby-genteel house for that new world they thrash out between them, fields of rock and guana where each household has its black servant –

'But no, that's not it at all,' Lili says, waking, 'he could never have been that soft-headed, besides he had a wife and child, the remains of a ceramics factory and stores for his delf in Dublin and London. All I know is that he would reappear on Bray prom at regular intervals with stool and canvas, to paint the same sea, the same line of hotels and his travels were much more local, I'd imagine, London, Paris and now and then Siena. And what's more he only took that last house when his wife had died, his son was on the point of marriage and the factory had closed for the seventh and final time. He still hopped from place to place, but in a smaller orbit, it was Sligo now, Clare, Portnu. He was taken in his own way by the peasant thing, the West, harsh rock and stone and whatever else. But not like his son, he still retained himself you see, I mean one is human, but one is either fish or fowl, an orgy of conscience and the assumption of a local accent doesn't help anyone, does it? No, the old man knew who he was, didn't have to learn Irish, amble into rooms with a look of pain in his face, photograph every Mick and Pat with snot on his nose and mud on his boots. I only knew him in the last three years as I told you, but he was leisured then, faintly privileged and knew it, lived on what he called "a fine trickle of dividends"' –

Walking through the Eucalyptus it begins to rain, slow straight threads of water, far apart at first, then more and more close, without any wind to impede its falling. A true downpour. He stands against a Eucalyptus, useless, since the leaves of that genus are tiny, a laughable contrast to the smooth sweep of its branch, its bark. He gets wet and the rain seems to hop from the ground and the strips of bark and the drops hop and turn to spray and the spray turns to mist. The air becomes fetid, the odour more than resinous, glue-like, as if the moisture clings to it and it to the moisture. He looks across the Bay and sees the impeccable sheen of the water, for once without colour of wind or current, made grey by the steady rain, an even sheet of hammered tin. The tart taste of bark in his mouth, his gums are hot and alive, the water pours down the skin of the trees unable to dim the cream-coloured peelings of bark which he sees for the first time as unlikely murals, scoured by some careless finger – whose? he wonders. He feels a life sleeping in him wakened by this odour of tropics. He thinks of the seed of this bark that travelled climates, sees a hill weeping in a blue haze, the huge trees dipping from it, losing their coats in long fleshly stripes. His tastes are mathematics and photography, his sympathies Republican, his background Protestant. He entered a Catholic marriage, his wife died, having borne him two sons. The self that watched, waited and observed seems to rear, now, like a tapeworm, pulled by this moisture through his opened lips. He looks at the plate of the sea and waits to see a face emerge, quietly, unheralded as if each detail was sculpted aeons ago like the faces that form themselves on the metal plates in his acid bath.

Would he ever see that face emerge? The meaning we demand from the span, the whole, but particularly from the surface frieze of the sensual world is never forthcoming, or if so not in any form that comforts. If it comes it is too late, if it speaks it is always in retrospect, the message he wants then from the grey sheet of sea and the tepid air comes only when both have been dulled by memory and time and quite another message is demanded, and besides by then the rain has stopped, the sea is quite achingly blue, washes another shore maybe, another bay and the only fresh shred that he retains is the one he never saw that edged into his picture from nowhere, with no reference to the real, that imagined hill with the tall trees in an outlandish climate, quite imaginary Eucalypti. And yet still it clung to him, a dogged belief in surfaces, he would have liked even then to photograph and capture that precise balance of elements, why the rain was on the sea, why the trees smelled and chanelled the water in sheets, perhaps even precisely for this reason – that tomorrow it might be blue and the air would contain nothing but the odour of sunlight, dust and sunlight. So that it could be held maybe, pasted in his black book on his green-felt table and seen as evidence of the impossibility of answers. '*How it was,*' each print would say, 'this is how it was on that day, the sun hit Luke's face in such and such a manner, he was seven then, already in braces –' 'Look,' another one said, 'this is Benburb Street in the days of hand-painted signs' and each print a document of *how*, a present that becomes past as soon as its developed and only through the future gradually reveals its real nature. The accumulation of them across years becomes a question-mark, a dogged, nagging why? Perhaps he suspected as he gathered them that each was the formulation of an ultimate question, each was a tentative attempt at it. But all answers aren't they retrospective? And it took stretches of days, months, years and prints for him to even realise what he was asking. Besides, he had a passive nature, paid obsessive attention to detail and suppressed the general, the kind of passive nature that when the rain stops falling round the Eucalypti walks away from them, stops thinking of them too.

IX
TEN POEMS

Sarah Lawson

Sarah Lawson was born in Indianapolis in 1943, and grew up in central Indiana. She studied English at Indiana University, where she took a BA in 1965. She holds an MA in English from the University of Pennsylvania and a PhD from Glasgow University, where her thesis was on Malory's *Morte Darthur*. She has written several notes and articles in scholarly journals and writes regularly for *New Library World*. Her poems have been published in a number of British and American magazines and journals including: *Critical Quarterly, English, The Friend, Orbis, Poetry & Audience, Workshop* and the Arts Council poetry anthology *New Poetry 4*. She is married and lives in London.

TEN POEMS

NOTES IN ADVANCE

I shall remind you of my death
Now when it seems far away.
I shall describe it
And what you will feel
And what you must avoid.
By saying all this now
Do I outwit the final silence?
Standing by my coffin,
You will know that
I've already shared this with you,
That I would comfort you now
But for this inconvenience.
I have done it in advance
As, going abroad in April,
We write notes in March
For the summer guests.

MUSICAL CHAIRS

The music is stopping, has stopped –
And only a sound ago the piano rang.
We are left without a chair
Where once a resonance past
There seemed so many.
While the chairless music played
Each fared as others fared;
Former comrades on their momentary seats
Forget the dispossession that we shared.

TWIDDLING THE WHEEL

Tomorrow might be several things
Or several other things.
Even the next hour has not happened yet.
We are always forming hours,
Like a potter never away from his wheel.
Say we carry a shaping wheel everywhere
Always with us, always twiddling it,
Pedalling at it, running wet fingers
Around the inside of slick hours.

FIFTEEN

Fifteen is a fitting room
Where we try on masks
In our search for a face –
A fitting room with a locked door
And no ventilation,
And on all sides imagined footfalls
Of indignant floorwalkers
Coming to investigate delay.

BOY DIVING

The diving board, hempen covered,
Bounces the confident
Into twelve clear feet of water.
The boy walks his plank, shivers,
Knows the older boys watch.
The rope beneath his feet
Licks like a lion's tongue;
At the end the water pauses
And waits with its mouth open.
He pictures in the air the shape he makes,
Then hides under the blue disturbance
To rise later, unconcerned, somebody else.

GIOTTO

Giotto drew a perfect circle once
To identify himself to strangers.
'Only Giotto could do this with his hand,'
They said, and straightaway believed.
The self he had accumulated
Since his birth was in his hands.
'I am Giotto.
Give me a pen or a piece of charcoal
And I will show you.'
They took a compass and fitted it to his line.
From an estimated centre the moving point
Followed close enough to Giotto's arc.
Sforza never believed anything at first
And carefully drew chords and bisected them
To find the centre. The compass now followed
Giotto's line exactly. When once Sforza
Thought he'd found a fault, Giotto showed him
Where his compass slipped.
Sforza folded the compass
And sat back sharply in his chair.
The name of Giotto and everything men knew
About him he could prove with one
Neat circling motion of his hand.
'I am Giotto. Let me draw
And I will prove it.'

VISIT TO A COTTAGE

With eyes that never need a magnifying glass
You examine window sills and lintels
Of this ordinary cottage
Half hidden from the traffic by some trees.
I stand beside you in your old boots,
Wondering how my week-end afternoons
Have turned so windy and mud footed.
Now like a horse dealer reading teeth
You finger over these roofless bricks,
And I, untrained in weathered brickwork, look at you.

I shall not write a monograph of findings;
I make no notes for lectures to the public.
I will keep this to myself:
How scuffing these wellingtons that you wore,
Slightly apart I watch and stand
As you touch a mouldered window, crazy door,
With your careful, uncommitted, ringless hand.

COLIN AT THE KEYBOARD

Somebody has emptied a fountain pen
On those pages –
I can see that from across the room.
And Colin, up to the knuckles in music,
Tries to get one hand free –
Three fingers free and then all of them –
To turn the page.
Quick as a shoplifter,
Colin turns the page and slaps it down
And the keys reclaim his hand.

THE PRESENT

The floor is not awake yet;
It is not ready to invite anyone to play on it –
No blocks and toy cars for another hour.
The woollen feet of her sleepers
Soften the antisocial floor
Before her mother swings her onto her shoulders,
Laughing, asking if she wants to see something –
Something left during the night. 'What? What?'
(A bit of artwork on the windows
Etched in the night by Jack Frost,
The noted cubist and colourist,
In his post-leaf phase, the early ice period.)
Back on the floor, stepping from foot to foot,
She sees the snowflakes like gummed-paper stars
Stuck all over the windows in the porch
(Sunny till bedtime summer porch!)

Porch as unfriendly as the floors.
Snowflakes stuck like bathroom glass,
Sprays of frozen ferns bouqueted but never grown.
And all left as a present for a child
Of a laughing mother with high connections.

GRAVEL PATHS IN KENTUCKY

'Well, Marquis,' said Daniel Boone,
'What brings you here?'

'I'm leaving my mistress.
I owe dinner parties to four hundred eighty-five people.
Have you ever owed intimate dinner parties
To four hundred eighty-five people?'

'Can't say as I have.'

'The Duc de Fromage cheated at cards
And claims I owe him nine thousand francs
Cash cheque or money order
"Choose your weapons," he said
But I never learned to shoot a pistol that well
And so I've come to be
An ex-marquis and wear fringe.
I hope I can have chamois gloves imported.'

'I reckon you come away 'thouten your musket.'

'I had no room for it.
I shall have someone else do my hunting,
Just as others prepare my food
And wash my linen and play my spinet.
That is no problem.
I am a marquis, you know.
Suppose I got calluses firing it?
Madeleine could never abide calluses
And I don't care for them either
I've seen them on outstretched hands
Vulgar palms wanting my silver
But think how ugly silver
And calluses would look together.'

'Sit down, brother, and take a cup of water.'

'Yes. Where? Oh here's a stump.
Very rustic. You have just cut down this tree,
Have you? How delightful. So pastoral.
My dear Daniel, I shall live here
In Kentucky
Without a mistress altogether
And go to operas only twice a month
I shall become a better man
I'm sure of it
And the fringe and so forth
It will change my appearance
Totally don't you think
I shall buy a different perruque.
These are really quite impenetrable woods,
Are they not, Daniel?'

'Don't see many folks by here.'

'Wonderful. I am a lover of solitude.
Trees and birds, you know.
Rabbits and so on. Squirrels.
Long walks through the gardens
I have not seen many gardens here
Is it so hard to find gravel
For the paths I wonder
Or have they not laid the pipes
For the fountains yet
I hope they hurry with the gardens
It is tiresome to have no place to walk.
My dear Daniel, I thank you for the water.
Please direct me to an auberge
Where I may further refresh myself.'

'There's a spring yonder, if you want another drink.'

'No, I mean an hôtel, an inn.
A shelter for weary travellers.
I am tired Daniel
I am not used to such exertion
I have been on that vulgar flatboat

All day and yesterday and before that
And only fish and pemmican to eat
But now I shall have lobster at the inn.
Where is the inn, Daniel?'

'There ain't an inn this side of the settlements.'

'Where do travellers stay, then?
They told me Americans were a little mad.
Milord, they said, don't go
You can go to Switzerland just as well
Or better
We will lie to the Duc de Fromage
Do not fear
But no I had to come
And now I've lost a buckle
And one stocking is ripped.
But Fromage will never find me.'

'You can stay in my cabin if you want to.'

'Daniel, at this point
I should not even mind your servants' quarters.
I shall move on of course
After one night
I must move on
How far is the sea
There is a large river first isn't there
I shall stop at the river
Perhaps there will be a château
(I grew up by the Loire, you know)
I shall find a turret – moats –
And settle down there.
Have you another chapeau like that?
Who is your hatter?'

'I make 'em as I need 'em.
It's easy done. I'll give you a coonskin.'

'That will quite change
The shape of my face, don't you think?
Even if I see Fromage

He won't recognize me
With one buckle and a torn stocking
Where is my snuff box
Daniel I want you to have this gold
Snuff box
It was a present from a lady
But no matter I am leaving all that
Please take it
My dear Daniel
I wanted to come for your war
With the English
But I couldn't get away
But now I'm feeling
Very revolutionary
The air here is much better
And beggars and cripples do not want your money.
Here Daniel my friend
Allow me to carry your axe
It is quite heavy
Oh I've ripped the other one
Yes you had better take it
I'm sorry Daniel
I shall learn about them in time
How far is it
Where is your carriage?
My dear Daniel, how long have you lived here
Without gravel paths?'

X
FOURTEEN POEMS

B.C. Leale

Photograph by Mark Gerson

B.C. Leale's first poem to appear in print was published in *The Observer* in 1961 and since then others have appeared in *The T.L.S., Tribune, Poetry & Audience, Ambit, Stand, Slow Dancer* and *The New York Times* amongst other British and American periodicals. His work has also appeared in several anthologies including *A Group Anthology*, of which Roger Garfitt, in an essay on 'the Group' in *British Poetry Since 1960*, said '... some of the liveliest contributions come from other poets – Rosemary Joseph, B.C. Leale, Margaret Owen – of whom one has heard too little since ...' This selection has been made to help redress the balance, because however many poems may appear separately, a reader can never really get an idea of a poet's work until a reasonable number are seen together. Other selections and single poem broadsheets available from small press publishers are *Under a Glass Sky*, 'Boarding House' and *Preludes* (all three from Caligula Books), 'Woman Alone' and 'Loaves' (both Mandeville Press) and 'Fouquet's' (Sceptre Press). B.C. Leale was born in 1930 and educated at the Municipal College, Southend. He is employed as a bookseller's assistant and lives in London.

FOURTEEN POEMS

VISIBLE WILDNOTES

The violin plays with a practised
sweetness a measured
smile of sound
that curves over the firmness of the bay

or it jags tinstrips
on dawn's dark
granite edges.

However, Heifetz
leaves the air
scored with black writhing fishes

goes out for a snack
or to write up his memoirs
or to crash the barriers of sound
in a jet that feathers down into Africa.
He hunts the last of the
visible wildnotes in the life-mask
of Stravinsky or merely

finds a locked room
in which he's sitting
in Paris in London in New York:
bullet/bone shield/brain/
high-pitched shearing/dismembering.

Heifetz listens at a lager glass
to a pacific
whisper of foam.

THE TRAPPING OF K

Her fleshiness and her sexuality with its regular
feeding times. The necessary sheet
of glass between them a great distance between cities
against which he presses. Writing with contorted urgency
in the shadow of a gold coil's suffocating touch
he speaks of the impossibility of their impending
lives together. He posts the letter and walks
out of the reptile house coughing up blood.

TENNESSEE WILLIAMS WRITES HIS MEMOIRS

Suite 229. The Excelsior Hotel on the Venice Lido.
It is three of the goddam morning. The light
smarts his sleepless eyes. The portable exposes
worn characters.

He kicks away fame. He kicks away critical works
and other eroding growths and says 'It is total
exposure. There are no half-truths.' He relives
disintegration. He suffers asylum walls
to give up their voices. He clings fast to a thread
that re-enters the blackest of convolutions.

Glare is intense in this room.
Glare dissolves the abrupt edges of furniture.
Glare is the furnace-fire of the man sitting typing.
Glare is the language of creation.

He sits by a swimming pool. He feels the flatness
    of failure.
Girls in bikinis have bared their lives.
They parade in all directions a single track.

HOMAGE TO MARCEL DUCHAMP/RROSE SÉLAVY

Rose

Please do not   ouch

Tired Old Man

Prune on the bed

Cowes

München

Moustached Sleepwalker

Whiskered away in the somnambulance

Le Petomane

Objet f'art

Hammer Horror Film

Hitting the head on the nail

Artistic Petrol

-ou have your (our) woo
-den floors polished with dental
manure it is enough to see glass fish hoo
-ks sink through folded con-
crete then to put newspaper grave
headlines into someone's un-
dissolved childhood. Fragments of anchored
whistles bubble out of our dullest
holly. Fossil Daimlers are dri-
ven out of the past tense of exhaust ex
-humed humour being its own dirigible

HAMPSTEAD PARISH CHURCH

There is this experimental graveyard
of moss, of aerial raindrops.
Tombstones struck
at arbitrary angles
grow lichen and such.
Near a brick wall Constable
is a chiselled name we come
amazed upon.
A little light leaks in
from a top corner of sky –
an early
watercolour.

FROGNAL WAY, N.W.3

You laugh
you jump up &
down in green-brown
rhythmic brush-strokes

you sense East Anglian
meadow-light
over the high brick
wall where
Constable
buried lyeth
in such a shining
of cleared sky.

SKETCH BY CONSTABLE

The dog knows it's an early draft. He's
full of destinations and joy as he
rounds the first bend from the house –
his shadow sharp, vibrant. Even the
path's edge is of frisky earth.

About five years later he's finished.
His short run by the water's edge completed and
he's famous. With muted shadow he looks up
to the men in a motionless hay-wain.

1828 – CONSTABLE'S WIFE DIES

Torn earth's debris of unleashed hedges
roars up. Rooks are a shrapnelling black.
A cottage that could open its door
slithers out of your grasp.
A track that could hold your feet
misfires into rock.
Flowers jet
shredding colours
in turmoiled oils. A great
contusion darkens the mind.

AIRPORT

Too much not wanting to be said
is in the slight tilting of a head.

Mollusc action of our lips –
protractiles of love perhaps.

Your plane now crazes the sky that yet
holds.

AT A PERFORMANCE OF JOHN CAGE'S *THEATER PIECE*, ROME 1963

A dead fish is flung into the piano
euphonious notes are a red herring.

PROPRIETOR

From the *Magnolia stellata*
a step to the waxed
white Cadillac.

ASCETIC

I

A full stop
in a glass box
preserves the
illusion

you have said something.

II

With a mental flurry
you pick off a feather
that ruffles the floor

the sky
returns to a
tidied silence.

CITY AT NIGHT

Darkness
with furniture
part of its
primaeval silence

the locked rooms
the cellular tissue
of the house
breathes and sleeps

bodies
no one possesses
fallen statuary
under sheets

embalmed
foetuses with their dreams
naked machinery left just
ticking over

down at street level
the array of names
fading
or freshly typed

a filing cabinet
of brick and mortar
a mortuary
of the still living

each body
on its temporary ledge
dipping into
an unfathomed blackness

in each stratified
house of each street
the overpowered
rapacious fauna

replications
in faint carbon
eight million abandoned lives sunk
in the primaeval silence.

A DREAM OF THE FILM LUIS BUÑUEL
NEARLY MADE

Light blossoming in corridors
of impenetrable carbon

from fossil clocks
the pale chiming of fish

a kerb encrusted suddenly
with a gold Lagonda

the announced princess wrapped in the white
hairy legs of an octopus

a table set with knives & more knives
& thickening with barbed wire

elsewhere lingerie trapped in the flow of volcanic mud
being freed by crucifixes of burnt fir.

XI
DEAD AND GONE
an extract

Sarah McCoy

Photograph by Martin Vaughn-James

Sarah McCoy (b. 1943) has lived in England, Australia, Canada and France and travelled widely in Western Europe, Central America and the U.S.A. In 1968 she left London and lived in Montreal for a time, after which she settled in Toronto for some years. During 1972-73 she lived in Paris where she first began to write seriously. Her work has been published in anthologies in Canada, and in 1976 her first short book, *Lies*, was published by the Dreadnaught Press. *Dead and Gone* is her first full-length novel and she is currently working on her second, with the aid of a grant from the Canada Council. Her major interest is French literature, in particular Proust, Céline, Beckett and the *nouveau romanciers*. She is married to the artist Martin Vaughn-James.

DEAD AND GONE

Truth is a pain which will not stop. And the truth of this
world is to die. You must choose: either dying or lying.

Louis-Ferdinand Céline

Author's Note

In my novel *Dead and Gone* textual motifs and structural themes are continuously reiterated throughout the entire narrative. Consequently any extract contains in part, or in microcosm, the essential motifs and themes explored elsewhere in the text. Since there is no 'plot', in the conventional linear sense of cause and effect, or any characterisation in the sense of psychological evolution or conflict, any attempt at synopsis must be directed towards the progressive and fragmentary accumulation of data (words) which actually constitute the novel itself. The very nature of these data is deliberately ambiguous, contradictory and suspect. For the sake of clarity, however, this flood of circumspect information can be seen to revolve around a series of supposed 'events'. (The essential ingredients of the narrative, like the events in Flaubert's *Madame Bovary*, are the stuff of pure melodrama – a murder, a wedding celebration, an inheritance, a party and a deathbed scene – in addition there is a certain amount of 'concrete evidence' – photographs, letters and cards – and the glue which binds all this together is the succession of voices which, in different ways, relentlessly pursue the 'Truth'.) This quicksand of facts and opinion is designed to pose more questions than answers. Or, more precisely, the text is continually posing questions to which it is the only answer.

S.M. 1977

when you think of how lovely it was there high up above the valley; see the houses nestling below the hollow of the hill a cool summer's afternoon in the middle of August little baby flowers peek-a-booing from under the soft mantle of the earth's green, nothing to do but lie back and enjoy it all and thank God for our blessings or what passes for them, near

enough is good enough you never miss ... but that's just
what they didn't think and that's what started them off on
what must have been a wild goose hunt, yes they were
searching alright and for that silly goose, the one they
figured would lay the golden egg or something resembling it
but who can possibly tell, were you there and can you read
peoples minds, how can you ever know, what are you
snooping for, aren't such things best left forgotten or unsaid
or something, if we go on this way there'll be no end to it
and it was so perfect there, close your eyes; the one you love
and are dreaming of in the winter by the fireside watching
the snow flakes glisten and seeing the sparks drift slowly
down from the treetops, the top storey the highest houses
the top of the hill the morning side of the mountain end of
story

but perhaps it might all have been different gone on for
ever if things had taken another turn entirely, there's no
harm done is there, we all have to go sometime and off they
went, not a chance from that point onwards to get a word in
edgewise and what else was there in the offing; she parked
herself in the corner quick smart, there was no budging her,
I thought we'd seen the last of her but there she was as bold
as brass her hat wedged onto her head as if it had been
there twenty years, her hair looked as if it hadn't seen a
comb for about the same length of time and the walk she'd
had hadn't helped, sweat from head to toe pouring off her,
it was in buckets, that handbag of hers looked as if it were
there to catch the drops, a horrible thing it was, a weird
shape I'd never seen one to match it and that dress, when
were they giving such things away, I'd run a mile not to be
so lucky, all in all a proper sight and playing the grande
dame if you please, just out for a stroll I don't think, she
hadn't come all that way on foot in that heat to pay us a
courtesy call I'll be bound, the best thing we could've done
was waited, sat on it a minute and waited for her to open
her Venus fly-trap but we were all so embarrassed by the
presence of number one, hadn't been seen outside her room
for something like a hundred years or as near as anyone
could remember, what was up we all thought but without
venturing to turn our heads, the road outside the window
dead silent, still and empty at that time of day, and as we

sat there kind of awkward not daring to take a squizz we suddenly saw the light play across it, dead peaceful it seemed you felt that it

we just wished but without saying it out loud the same thought on everyone's mind, there but for the grace of God ... lying on top of a mountain in the warm soft sunlight feet up taking it easy let someone else do all the work, what's in it for number one ...

great minds think alike that's probably what they thought when they put their heads together, two heads better than one but in this case it was difficult alright, no two ways about it, best to stay out of sight till the whole thing blows over, it's been going on long enough and if we weren't so scared about the whole nasty mess we'd be bored stiff with it, but never had any sense and there was no getting out of it now ... if only it hadn't started, had never been ... but there's no use wishing, sighing and whining and making a fuss, just got to get on with it and make the best of it and to cut a long story short make an end of it

dirty work was afoot oh, very wise after the fact but first let's get the facts, gather ye rosebuds and get the evidence together, can't do it on your one and only it's not humanly possible, a mountain of facts got to keep a sharp lookout

from the highest branches spreading slowly no stopping it not for all the tea in China; we didn't lift a finger

in the top storey spinning a tall story whiles away the hours something to do life obliges us to do something, anything, what was it to be, neither fish nor fowl, obliged to go on, carry it a stage further, all the time one eye open the thing taking wing rising slowly, higher ground, the untrodden path, the end of the line, how shall I say it ... the finish

the screaming finish as plain as the nose on your face, should've seen it coming, brewing for a long time bad blood there, no stamina, there's a word for it I believe but the worse thing was the stain, it really raised a stink, not in our part of the country, in our neck of the woods, had we known anything like it since ... but that must have been nigh on twenty years ago if it was in living memory at all, but there was no use crying over spilt milk or blood or whatever, the question was how to go on a day at a time knowing in advance sensing the waste the futility the fading strength the ebbing purpose it was quite ridiculous these ideas these images ... love friendship the rest of that rot

it's an ill wind that blows ... in that part of the country especially at that time of the year and on the night in question it was howling fit to split your eardrums, yes the noise was terrific really something colossal, which was why when we heard that they reported having heard footsteps in the drive two by two one slowly silently after the other we thought well, there's more here than meets the eye, at that time of night with all that going on too, if there's any truth to the story, more likely a pack of old wives tales but ... embarrassed, I should say so, what with all those fairy lights the band a racket to wake the dead and packed to the rafters with strangers of every description a very motley collection couldn't spell half their names let alone pronounce them, we'd never heard the like, such goings on and such types, so it's no wonder is it that when you know who turned up like that right out of the blue or rather the drizzle, coming down in buckets it was at that point, that they stood there stunned you might say, a nasty shock, the bad penny the ugly princess the wicked fairy come to ... uninvited and unwanted but there in the flesh ... put a jinx on the festivities what were they in aid of, a premonition or something of the sort, they stood on chairs and what have you to get a better look threw open the windows all over the house unwise under the circumstances if you see what I ... because after all, a perfect right more than most and no two ways about it, just carried away swept along in the general feeling of horror revulsion shame but had to carry on to make the best of it, a bad lot a bad bunch would all end up on the gallows and make a bad end of it if they could carry on ... with it, the business in hand I'm referring to; unattended, a complete farce the whole affair hushed up the main points forgotten or the issues laid to rest and about time too, let's get on with it though or the gist of it will escape us entirely; not much to tell you never know the other chap's point of view no use worrying your head over such trifles is there

gone and forgotten sounds words carried by the wind whispered in the trees heard on forgotten roads on the

corners of empty streets deserted places themselves
forgotten and silent ashes to ashes and dust to

plenty more where that came from, no end to the
mischief some people will do if left to their own devices, as if
they were blameless or had nothing better to do but
probing prying, noses always in other peoples business,
intrigues plots hatching scheming, the throat as dry as a
bone with all this everlasting talking gossiping conniving,
and in the middle of it a real hornet's nest a spider's web of
untruth and supposition, the grave to end it all, to cap it off
nicely for them, waiting in the wings

a whole row of them swaying gently to and fro
murmuring and nodding heads together tall and straight
when they were still which wasn't often at that stage, just
shapes and nothing more, hard to make out anything in
that murk, row upon row, been there a long time, hushed
and brooding, as long as well, living memory anyhow, and
all in line a guard of honour you might say like sentries or
something of the sort, the clouds forming a series of hoods
over their heads like cowls as if they were in mourning for
what and for whom and since time immemorial; at the end
the lights a sense of warmth in that, a kind of promise but
that a delusion, no sanctuary there or anywhere for that
matter, their moaning rising and becoming a kind of hymn
and below them their feet buried in it every one, gravel,
nothing but trees, inanimate, they can't speak, everyone in
their right mind knows that, why it's elementary, so it must
have been madness loneliness or something so like it that
you can only guess at it, nothing but a bit of gravel and a
few tall trees and at the end of it quite an ordinary house,
not a bungalow but the next best thing, certainly nothing to
write home about at least not without a good deal of
embroidering on the basic facts but it all helps to pass the
time, to keep going from one day to the next not much
difference between them, one and the next, might have been
could have been why bother to make such a fuss about it,
anyway no harm done, all ship-shape and Bristol fashion or
near enough as makes no distance, no, that's not it at all, it
wasn't like that, not the least bit

hot, a straggly hedge and a short path right to the back
door the tradesman's entrance, yes they went in for that in

a big way, nothing like it for sorting out the men from the boys the haves and the have-nots, not that it makes the least bit of difference in the end; shod barefoot or what have you you have to get there somehow and on time, there's no waiting of that you can rest assured, it's you or the next man but it's someone or other for sure ... as a matter of fact it could be you

safe and sound right on time not a minute to spare

it couldn't wait, they had all night, take your time all the time in the world but nowhere to go they couldn't leave even if they got there, that wasn't the purpose of the exercise, just keep going step by step and in the end nothing, blackness, silence, a line of whispering mouths, trees overhead an avenue of honour flashing steel swords scabbards an arch of triumph or something that stood in lieu of same, and the feet one two or many making their way on the gravel hurrying rushing on gravel-voiced, the eyes grave and solemn, lighted at the end the first time we caught sight a port in the storm

slammed on the brakes foot to the floor what a clamour and a shake up, over in a minute the beginning of the end, head over heels the lot of them, too many to begin with all jam-packed in their ... what were they up to; the devil takes care of his own ... thrown clear of the thing that time, as well there was no one about or innocent people could've been hurt, maimed mutilated scarred for life, a thing like that a freak of nature at that time of the year the season of plenty and not a soul ... insight is what's called for but the last thing in the world they possessed was a bit of consideration for others so we thought; with all their gadgets their what-nots it was too much to fathom at least for the likes of us but we'd have liked some had we had half the chance; concrete all around not a blade of grass for miles a huge monster of a place a real barn a warren if you please, these new-fangled ideas, block of flats not good enough for them, a duplex a maisonette a high-rise a black wart that's what it was and they made a nice mess of it horrible as it was to start with; hit the marble pillars the plush entrance hall at a smart trot, chandeliers in all directions settees with their insides ripped out, a mass of splintered wood chipped teeth shredded limbs and missing knives and forks; who lived there in those days, did they voluntarily move in to such a place, was it on a trial basis, or was it after a trial of some sort as some kind of punishment, a gaol then, and if that was the way things were not much of a picnic after all and maybe that explains the whole thing in the first place; why have you wasted so much valuable time and energy getting this far, I doubt it was worth it, the thing's cut and dried and you should have realised that in the beginning, nothing new under the sun the same old story a hundred times repeated and repeated till we could all scream and recite it by heart; start again at the beginning

a quick wash and brush up and right as rain again time to get going again the main thing's to keep on the go live longer tell the tale

small pieces words chips fragments but enough to make something of it in the gloom, it won't lift, too heavy now, too long weary worn tired ... used up the first hundred times; the speed, it's surprising, soon there, no trouble just keep going it couldn't be as far as it seemed, the horizon on the left the birds a bit late I'd have thought, a sense of relief not much further, it was what we were all looking for at that stage, at one time, and not long ago ... but even then when we heard about it you couldn't say the facts and we'd forgotten all about the truth by that ... well, there's a limit to everything and all we wanted was a respite; in short we'd had enough, it had turned out rather badly we thought, that was the general consensus

over and done with make a clean break that was the best idea by far, it would've been a very good thing if we'd taken our own advice yet even that would have been far from sufficient to still the wagging tongues the malice of the uninformed, virtuous all right, and always the ones to point the way ... clear out they yelled we thought we'd seen the last of your decrepit carcasses around here but no one was to be seen, they'd all gone long ago, the dear departed, you never miss them till you don't have them or is it simply that they're not around, yes but not within earshot so it amounts to the same thing; alone and afraid of being forgotten or interrupted or both, it's the same thing, just yapping on everlastingly about something unimportant something nobody's interested in, they've never heard of it, all that's ancient history; so they lost a few arms and legs a few hundred teeth got smashed what's it to number one; we're all in the same boat at eventide alone on a deserted road in the middle of the ocean an ocean of souls and not a drop to drink; it's all very well to say take your pick hold your tongue hang fire, that's not what pays the bills, things are a little more complicated than that, it'd be a lovely to do if we just sat and thought about justice and what have you but someone's got to get on with it, the work I mean, and who's got time to sit and jaw all bleeding day especially about a load of old rubbish that didn't serve to interest decent law-abiding folk when it was red-hot news if it ever was and not just a little device of you know who; I wouldn't put it past you to have dreamed the whole thing up yourself, why don't you come right out and admit it's all your own doing, you've carried it this far let us in on the joke

someone told me that they saw her and that she was right all along, on to it from the start, the only one to scent the danger right behind her

went to powder her nose, not that it needed any more muck on it, and I wouldn't be at all surprised to find that it was precisely at that moment coming up the long weed-choked drive, a mass of growth prickles and thorns, that she made a dash for it through the back window, the one they normally keep locked, so that while we were all waiting out front expecting her to reappear any minute through the long glass door who should come sneaking through an upstairs window, the one they'd left open to air on account of the wet wash that just wouldn't dry because of the clammy weather we'd been having at that time, so unnatural, not at all what you'd expect

with our backs to the whole thing gradually spreading up the road as if ... and it seems nothing better to do; honest, upstanding, chairs, anything they could find

a few fingers missing you don't need both hands to open a window that's been left gaping like an open mouth, I could have said you know what but it wouldn't be nice not kind let alone refined; behind us from the rear, God help us what next, Martians without heads in the next world, they came into this one bawling without an invitation and went out as silent as the grave; can't you leave it alone, let it be, none of our business what's it to us; I don't know it makes me nervous just to think about such a thing and right in our midst as plain as ... beings the same as ... except for the deformities but we hadn't eyes then it was all hidden in the mists of time

a bright light shone all eyes were rivetted on the glass a screen on which the figures came and went, she'd gone alright taken off, how's that for trust and devotion and so forth, left standing for all our pains, only the sign – thumb your nose when you say you've gone to powder it – Ladies Room Women Only Dames or Damas something unfamiliar, it's not done, but over and done with long ago just a waste of time trying to go over it now, may as well try walking on the moon but then that's been done now hasn't it, is nothing sacred; dead scared we heard the sound we all dreaded most right over our shoulders; throw some for luck and see if that helps

wanting wishing pretending that's all very well but how about settling down to some hard work the facts or as near – but that won't do – there must be, and if only ... but it's not a question of that, not by a long shot

left without the time of day and wouldn't give it to you not that we thought she'd ever had it or even a look in but they were convinced otherwise and that's where it all started the hoopla and hanky-panky

a moth-eaten old fur cat or some such mangy beast of the same family you'd wonder that such well brought-up toffee-noses such swells would let one of their own while there was still food on the table, when the ink wasn't yet dry on the papers, yet up she comes bold as brass in full view of the assembled one heel broken, dragging herself as if on her last leg, had a drop too many slurring it I bet though no one heard; crash of brakes, family shame heirlooms the lot all wiped out, a few bottles broken, splattered and plastered and naught to say once it was done and well over with

fine lace hand-sewn hems nothing too good for the favourite it didn't seem right, could do no wrong, as if the fairy princess the delight of all – welcome all everyone welcome – everywhere right at home; hat in hand down and out dejected forgotten dismissed; is it any wonder then a

quick nip now and again helps you get on with it can't stop
once you've started didn't wait to be asked twice, wasn't
there in the first instance

but what started it all the shame and sorrow that
wouldn't stop wouldn't go away ... why was the old girl ...
her unexpected visit yes, what had she come to say after all
that time and distance blood thicker than water and wine
too for that matter, dirty work was afoot to be sure, it's like
the other one had always said empty hands tempt the devil
there's nothing truer than that you can say it's only words
but I know different

or was it that she said keep your hands to yourself a wife
in every port that's all very well but I've better things to do
with my time, walks at dusk along deserted country roads
windows open to catch the last of the sun's rays the warmth
of day fading fast the birds getting ready for the night tuck
themselves up in their little nests a bit of shut-eye not a
bird's eye view of the world a nice safe narrow life
uncomplicated no surprises but no catastrophes either,
which would account for her surprise then when looking
out the window, the one on the top floor at the back
overlooking the lane, and having a fine view of the hill from
the top of which at that hour of the day it is possible that
someone could, with the aid of a good pair of binoculars or
armed with second sight so to speak, observe the goings on
down below as well as if the sun was in the right part of the
heavens and the moment opportune, very likely, if you
understand my meaning

could it have been on the other hand that the beginning
of all the misery was that harmless card, we never did get to
the bottom of that did we, what kind was it, some said a
birthday card others a card of condolence but I heard from
the horse's mouth so to speak that it was nothing less than a
declaration of well, perhaps a Valentine's Day greeting of
some kind, which was quite out of the question seeing that
there never was a more unpopular girl, a regular plain
Jane; was the mother surprised, I can't see how it could be
otherwise unless the whole thing was sent for her benefit to
make her feel that the little beast the ugly duckling wasn't
as bad as all that; there are plenty of fish in the sea and
more than ever came out of it, the poor thing hardly her

fault if she's been saddled in life with a face like the back of
a bus but very strange all the same considering the
circumstances, the parents the father, oh very pleased with
himself, a regular good-looker or so his mirror told him and
he spent enough time in front of it, meticulous he was, and
spare the rod his motto, trimming his little waxen
moustache just like a woman every little stray hair, the
eyebrows tweezed regularly, they couldn't be accused of …
yet people will talk … empty vessels, we'd been warned but
do you ever learn or profit by experience

how could we know where it came from who posted it or
when it was sent, one thing's for certain it arrived right on
the day, neither early nor late, there was some mystery
about it even at the time people wondered did he, the father
that is, the brother of the other one, send it or had the son,
the brother of the uncle, sent it when he was out of town
and calculated the day and the time having pity on the poor
thing, the sister that is, because after all it wasn't her fault
she wasn't to blame one of Nature's little mishaps; a fine
looking lad the talk of the town even though we had no idea
then of what it would mean and the mother, she hopped
into the act always ready to steal the limelight take the
credit and bask in reflected glory, all of a sudden it was my
darling daughter this the fairy princess that enough to turn
your stomach what a display really, some people, have they
no shame no sense of decency; it could have been anyone at
that time of the year there are plenty of people around and
it would have been fairly easy for someone, a passing fancy,
ships that pass in the night, and then the stab of remorse
later the little pang of conscience was that it, no more to it
than that … we wondered, but has the cat got your tongue
you haven't said a word for ages, what's your opinion of the
affair if that's in fact what it was and if so then that would
explain how the whole other business got going and came
into being, it would furnish a kind of motive for such an act
which otherwise must remain quite outside the bounds of
reason, an unmentionable thing

others said that years later when it had all blown over
and cooled down completely the girl herself came forward
and as good as admitted – that's to say she might as well
have confessed – that she posted the card in question to

herself or got one of her girl friends to do it for her from the next station down the line from the stop where she, the girlfriend, lived, so as to divert suspicion and that she, the girlfriend again, didn't know what she was up to and just did it to oblige her, she was always getting strange ideas she said she'd done it to make her mother happy so that they, the parents, wouldn't think that she was such a booby and a lame duck and despair of her ever ... and put her away in a place for girls like that, a convent it was whispered; had she a vocation, a persecution complex, or was it religion, some kind of mania or neurosis for which there was no cure, what else could they do only walk at sunset in the twilight and what have you

a sorry story morose and morbid fretful and fierce a fine how-d'ye-do and was it gradually getting worse or were we to hope for something better, a break in the clouds a ray of sunshine on the thorny path

some said the whole thing could be put down to passion or something of the sort but we wondered what kind could that old body be capable of, not that she was really old mind, but with her lack of opportunities not to mention graces or beaux or good looks it just seemed that way; no one was interested of course, after all what was there of interest to anybody in their right mind about the child, and when I say child I mean she must have seen a bit of water flow under the bridge, perhaps that accounted in part for the bitterness, a polite word for such nastiness, a face to match her nature, one of Nature's mistakes or perhaps that's too strong a word mistake, error call it, I mean her, it was a crying shame a dreadful cross to bear, you can understand given the circumstances how that would account for ... but can you possibly excuse such a thing, I know where I stand wasn't it rather the fault of the whole lot of them; after all they started it spread the rumours truth or lies it was all fuel for the flames

it simmered poisonous and uncontrolled hatred pure and simple it can drive you mad, dive in and you're up to your precious neck in it there's no escape and soon you don't want any, you've forgotten such an alternative exists, insatiable and irreversible, dangerous at times, the worst of other things passes but not this, it accumulates with speed

gets a good move on in times of sickness and health there's
always something to curse, go on have your say yell and
scream try and get it out of your system it does no good,
there's no getting away from it, it's come to keep you
company adhered itself cold and slimy or hot and vicious,
either way you've got it for keeps wearing itself out on this
one leaving you drunk and demoralised then on to the next
but improving, gaining strength as you lose what's left of
yours ... had you any to start, anything but this, soon it's
hard to imagine life without it, the passion, the hatred I'm
talking about ... still on about it after all this time a lot of
water must've

the tragedy in our midst, strikes you down without
looking, and in the prime of life if you could grace it with
such a word, was there ever anything to compete with it ...
the sheer gall of the woman after all they'd said about the
old harpie ... sitting there good as gold in the middle of the
afternoon as if nothing had happened or was about to
happen, over in the corner and not a peek out of her, tea for
one and buttered scones a little jam too I think, bold as
brass quiet as a mouse all eyes turned away, we gazed out
onto the road had our backs turned one and all as if she'd
ceased to exist, a hundred miles away you might say, little
suspecting ...

XII
THE KASSANDRA PENINSULA

Concerning certain ambiguities
in the life and character of
Miss Una Persson

Michael Moorcock

Photograph by Colvin

Michael Moorcock was born in London in 1939. He is the editor of *New Worlds* and has written some forty popular 'fantastic' romances and various 'experimental' novels (including the highly praised Jerry Cornelius tetralogy, of which the last part, *The Condition of Muzak*, has recently appeared in paperback). He has performed with the rock band Hawkwind and plays his own compositions with the band Deep Fix. His most recently published book is *Gloriana: or the unfulfilled Queen* (Alison & Busby) and he is currently working on a book and record album featuring Una Persson, to be called *The Entropy Tango*.

THE KASSANDRA PENINSULA

Concerning certain ambiguities
in the life and character of
Miss Una Persson

> *In which his torment often was so great,*
> *That like a Lyon he would cry and rore,*
> *And rend his flesh, and his owne synewes eat.*
> *His own dear* Vna *hearing euermore*
> *His ruefull shriekes and gronings, often tore*
> *Her guiltlesse garments, and her golden heare,*
> *For pity of his paine and anguish sore;*
> *Yet all with patience wisely she did beare;*
> *For well she wist, his crime would else be neuer cleare.*

Spencer, *The Faerie Queene* (I.x.28)

I

Una Persson considered her compact. It was silver, with
delicate enamel-work by Brule; one of his last pieces.

'Una.'

She shook her head. She refused his confession. His eyes
were agony.

'Una.'

She replaced the compact, unused, in her patent leather
purse.

'Una.'

He lay in the shadows, on straw. Through the barn door
came the hard air of the New Hampshire winter. She could
see across the deep, undulating snow the outlines of a
Dutch farmhouse, black against the near-white sky, the
isolated birches, the clustering pines; she could hear the
muffled sounds of work. It would be dawn in a moment:
they would discover him soon. Freezing her face, Una
forced herself to look at him.

'Una.'

One hand moved a fraction. She glanced beyond his head, at the disused harness, the rusty implements: mementoes of simpler days. She smoothed the silk of her skirt and swung the purse by its strap; then she put it over her shoulder.

'Una. They'll kill me.'

'No.' He would probably be interned until after the primaries. She was close to offering reassurance when happily there came a scream from the sky and snow thudded from the roof of the barn as a pirate Concorde passed overhead, pursued by angry Freedom Fighters. It was so cold and she had no appropriate clothing. 'Montreal,' she said. 'Try to get to Montreal. I'll see you there.' She stepped in black high-heeled court shoes into the snow. She shuddered. It was stupid to have trusted the old Kamov.

II

'We begin with ambiguities and then we strive to reconcile them through the logic of Art,' said Prinz Lobkowitz. 'Though these chaps often begin with some simple idea and then try to achieve ambiguity through obfuscation. It won't do.' He threw the composition paper on the floor beside the piano and got up. 'I blame the academics.'

'Well,' she said, 'it's easy.'

She leaned back on the piano stool and swung round to peer at the half-built auditorium. She could see the night sky through the gaps in the tarpaulings covering the shattered glass of the dome; another publicist's broken dream. Lobkowitz, in evening dress, loped forward, tall and thin, looking less well than usual. His attempt, at the invitation of the United States provisional government, to form a cabinet had failed, as he had guessed it would. As a result both he and Una were out of a job. She was relieved; he was contemplative. The meeting, which had been held earlier that evening, in the light of candles and oil-lamps, had taken on the air of a funeral reception. Then, gradually, the distinguished old men had drifted away. All but a few of the lamps were out. It was a shame that the damp had affected the murals, from Mozart to Messiaen, on the hastily emulsioned walls. She appreciated the peculiarities of Gregg's style, with its muted colours and shadowy outlines. She had particularly liked the portrait of Schoenberg, on stage for *Pierrot Lunaire* in Berlin, 1912. Now, however, only the composer's raised hands were perceptible, as if he conducted the invisible crowd, here muting the antagonist shouts, there bringing up the applause. Una wished she could explain her sudden feeling of well-being. She swung to smile at Lobkowitz who shrugged, grinning back at her. 'Ah, well.'

III

Reluctantly she picked up the Ak-47 as Petrov pushed pouches of ammunition across the table at her.

'It suits you,' he said. 'It's elegant, isn't it?' He lit a thin cigar. 'You know the rifle?'

'Oh, yes.' She checked its action. 'I was hoping I'd never see one again.' The smoke from his cigar made her feel sick.

'There's the M-60 ...' He made a movement towards the rack.

'No, no.' She clipped the pouches to the webbing of her lightweight camouflage jacket. She wished that she didn't feel quite so comfortable in the gear. It was suspicious. Another cloud of smoke reached her face. She turned away.

'You have everything else?' he asked. 'Plenty of mosquito oil?'

'Plenty. Can't you tell?' She wiped her fingers over the back of her greasy wrist.

He stood up. 'Una.'

'Oh, no you don't,' she said. Helping the wounded was not part of her brief.

'It's you I'm thinking of.' He sat down again, staring beyond her at the veldt on the other side of the border. He brightened, pointing. 'Look. Vultures.'

She did not turn.

He was grinning. 'They're a protected species now, you know.'

Carefully she closed the screen door behind her and stood on the veranda, looking up the road for her transport. It was already half-an-hour late. She wondered if something had happened to it. If so, it would mean a long wait while they radioed back to Kinshasa for instructions. She glanced at her watch without reading it. She had never been over-fond of Africa. Somehow, in spite of everything, they had continued to look to Europe for their models. Just like the Americans. And here she was, Britannia Encyclopedia, returned for the shoot-out.

'You 'ave to larf, don't you, Miss?' said the black cockney corporal, holding up the water-can in which someone had shot two small holes. His heavy boots made the veranda shake as he went by, entering Petrov's office to request an order.

She sat down in a khaki deck-chair, placing the rifle at her feet. She stretched her body. The corporal came out again. 'Seen anything of that Captain Cornelius, Miss?' he asked, to pass the time. ''E was 'ere before the real trouble started.'

She laughed. 'He usually is.'

IV

As the river broadened, she became alert, releasing the safety catch, crouching in the front of the motor launch and studying the jungle. She gave particular attention to the thicker clumps of reeds on both banks. She made out the funnels and bridge of the old steamer which had been ambushed here two years before. It had keeled over so that it was almost on its side. As she watched, a small crocodile emerged from one of the funnels and wriggled into the water. There was a horrible silence in the jungle, as if every bird and insect had been blown away. Yet the foliage itself was lusher than ever; fleshy and dark green. They approached a bend. A huge stretch of dirty detergent scum came swirling towards them and passed on both sides of the labouring launch. In the stern Shaky Mo Collier was jumping up and down throwing carved wooden idols into the scum. 'Fuck you! Fuck you!' He drew the idols from a bulky sack, almost as large as himself. He had been upset to learn that his 'loot' had become valueless since the falling off of the tourist trade.

The jungle on the right bank ended suddenly to be replaced by the great grey terraced complex of Durango Industries' protein processing plant. Nearby were the white buildings of the hospital, identified by their red crosses, looking remarkably like reception buildings for the plant. Workers on the roofs and gantreys paused to watch the launch. Shaky Mo Collier waved at them but lost interest when nobody waved back. 'Surly buggers,' he complained.

He moved along the deck to stand beside her. 'There won't be trouble here, will there?'

'Unlikely.' She wiped her forehead. 'The worst is over. It seems we'll be slipping this shipment through, at least.'

'I'm making bloody sure I get my bonus in my hand next time.' Mo scowled. 'In gold.' He patted his belt pouch. It bulged. From under the tightly buttoned flap a few hairs emerged.

Una still marvelled at Mo's ability to adopt enthusiastically the ideals and ambitions of any employer. Asked about this he had replied: 'I like being loyal.'

He had earned his high reputation in Africa. She nonetheless enjoyed his company and would be sorry to part, but with the successful delivery of their cargo her mission would be over. She was glad the journey had been relatively swift. No amount of disinfectant or perfume could disguise the smell from the hold. It was the last time, she promised herself, that she did a job for Cornelius. Collier could continue with the load to Dubrovnik if he wanted to, but she had had enough.

V

'Of course, I remember him from the early, carefree days,' said Miss Brunner, smiling up at the crystal ball which turned in the centre of the ceiling of Lionel Himmler's Blue Spot club. 'He was much better company, then.' She seemed to be implying that that was before he had met Una. There was nothing superficially attractive about the woman, in her severe suit; her awkward, almost self-conscious, way of moving; but Una experienced a strong desire to make love to her, perhaps because she sensed no hint of resonance, no sympathy for Miss Brunner. She tried to suppress the thought; she had a good idea of any consequences resulting from even a brief affair. 'When he was still idealistic, I suppose,' continued Miss Brunner. 'Weren't we all?'

'I still am,' said Una. 'It's silly isn't it?' She was shocked at herself. That last remark was unlike her. She admired Miss Brunner's power to produce it.

Miss Brunner gave her a smile which might have been of sympathy or triumph. 'When you're as old a campaigner as me, dear, you won't have time for that sort of thing.' She signed to the sour-faced Jewish waiter. As he approached she pressed a coin into his hand. 'Bartok's String Quartet No. 1,' she said. She watched him shuffle towards the juke-box. It was her turn to display embarrassment. 'I'm feeling a bit reflective. You weren't about in the old days, of course.'

'It depends what you mean,' said Una.

'Our paths hadn't crossed, at any rate.'

'No.' Una wondered how, with so many wounds, the woman could continue to function.

Miss Brunner sipped her B&B. From the fur collar of her jacket came the smell of artificial hyacinths. 'It's nice to know someone's prepared to fill in for him.'

'I'm not exactly filling in,' said Una. 'I think you have the wrong impression.'

'That's what they told me at the Time Centre.'

'Auchinek?'

'No, the other one. Alvarez.'

'He only enjoyed working with Cornelius.'

'That's true.'

'Of course you move about more than any of us ever did, don't you?' Miss Brunner continued.

'I suppose I do.'

'I envy you your freedom. I'm afraid I'm very old fashioned.'

Una was amused by the series of ploys. 'Oh, no,' she said.

'A terrible reactionary, eh?'

'Not at all.'

'I came out of a very different school.' Reminiscently Miss Brunner smacked her lips.

'It's just a question of temperaments,' said Una.

'Well we each of us see what we're looking for. Especially in a man. That's what "knowing" someone means, doesn't it?'

The waiter returned, just as the scratched record began to play.

'I hate Bartok.' Miss Brunner picked up the menu. 'I find him empty. Vivaldi's what I really like, but the selection's so limited here.' She peered savagely up at the waiter. 'I'll have the moules to begin.'

'They're Danish,' said the waiter.

'That's right. And then the jugged hare.'

'Just an omelette.' Una made no attempt to read the menu in the dim light. 'And some mineral water.'

'Plain omelette? Perrier?'

'Fine.'

'Anyway,' said Miss Brunner as she handed the menu to the waiter, 'Collier got through with that last consignment. Which about wraps Africa *and* South America up.'

'It's a relief.'

'It must be for you. I'll be going back to Sweden tomorrow. It's where I live now.'

'Yes.'

'You know Sweden?'

'Oh, yes.'

'Kiruna?'

'Yes.'

'It's so peaceful.'

Una could not bring herself to confirm any of these desperate affirmations. As a result Miss Brunner became agitated and cast about for another weapon.

'He was never straightforward,' she said at length. 'That's what I couldn't stand.'

'Well, some of us need to create an atmosphere of ambiguity in which we can thrive.' Una hoped the response wasn't too evidently direct.

'I don't quite follow you, dear.' Miss Brunner had understood all too readily.

Una dispensed with caution. 'While others of course try to resolve something from the ambiguity they sense around them. As I say, it's a matter of temperament.'

'It's obvious which kind of temperament meets with your approval.'

Una smiled. 'Yes.'

'Speaking for myself, all I want is a quiet life. You didn't get that with Cornelius. He'd foul anything up.'

'I probably didn't know him as well as you did.'

'Very few people could have done.'

Miss Brunner's mussels arrived. She bent her angry head over the bowl. ,

VI

It was a relief to get into the car and stuff Ives's First Symphony into the player. It wasn't that she had objected to the Bartok, but Himmler's ancient recordings, always too heavy on the bass and worn and scratched, made everything sound awful. Of course Himmler regarded even this as a concession. When he had opened the nightclub there had been nothing but Phoenix records to play – a label devoted entirely to Hitler's speeches and National Socialist songs. It had been founded by Arnold Leese, best remembered for calling Mosely a 'Kosher Fascist'. This description was more appropriate to Himmler himself who had, in 1944, changed his name from Gutzmann. It was amazing, she thought, as the music began, how she was warming to America since it had rejected her.

She drove through a cleaned-out Soho, her body filled with sound from the quad speakers in the AMC Rambler Station Wagon she currently favoured. She had never been happy with non-automatics, and though this car had seen more exciting days it provided a secure environment in a world which, at present, she preferred for its chaos. The alternatives to chaos were all too suspect. With the volume as high as possible it was impossible to hear either the engine, the air-conditioning or the few other noises from the streets. This and her sound-proofed flat helped her keep herself to herself. Just now, she had no time for civilians or casualties. The abandoned strip-joints and casinos behind her, she made for Hyde Park as the second movement began. It was hard to believe that this was the conception of a seventeen-year-old. She yearned for her lost youth.

Studying her hands as they rested casually on the large steering wheel she almost crashed into the pack of dogs crossing the road in front of her. The dogs were the reason why it was now only safe to drive through the park. Mongrels, greyhounds, alsatians, chows and poodles ran erratically, snapping at one another's necks and flanks, and disappeared into the shrubs. She turned out of the park into Bayswater Road, passed Notting Hill Gate and the ruins of the apartment buildings blocking Kensington Park Road, made a right into Ladbroke Grove then, eventually, another right into Blenheim Crescent, stopping outside the seedy terraced house she feared so much, even though it sheltered at least one of the people she loved.

She disembarked from the car and locked it carefully, putting the keys into the pocket of her long black trench-coat. She turned up her collar, mounted the cracked steps, found the appropriate bell and pressed it. She leaned on the door, watching the Co-op milkman as his van moved slowly down the other side of the street making deliveries. Una pressed the bell again, knowing that there was bound to be someone up. It was almost seven o'clock. There was no reply. The milkman came back along the other side of the road. Una pressed the bell for the third time. The milkman climbed the steps with five pints in his arms. He set them at her feet. 'You're up early,' he said. 'Who you after?'

'Cornelius,' she said.

He laughed, shaking his head as he went away.

Una found his attitude irritatingly mysterious and would have followed him to question him had not she heard a cautious movement on the other side of the door. She stepped out of view, huddling against the broken pillar of the porch. The door rattled. It opened a fraction. A red hand reached for the milk.

'Good morning,' said Una.

The hand withdrew, but the door did not shut.

'Mrs Cornelius?'

'Not in,' said an unmistakable voice. 'Bugger orf.'

'It's Una Persson.'

The door opened wider and Mrs Cornelius stood there, in curlers, her woolly dressing gown drawn about her, her bleary eyes blinking. 'Ha!' she said. 'Thort you woz ther bleedin' milkman.' Now Una knew why he had laughed. It was why there had been no answer to the bell – the combination of bottles rattling and the doorbell ringing sent Mrs Cornelius automatically to cover. 'Wotcha want?'

'Actually I was looking for Catherine.'

'Actcherly, she ain't 'ere.'

Mrs Cornelius relented. 'Orl right, luv, come in.' She took two pints from the step, darted a look along the street, admitted Una, closed the door.

Una followed Mrs Cornelius, ascending stone stairs still bearing traces of broken linoleum; they reached a landing and a half-open door. She entered a room full of unattractive smells – cabbage, lavender water, beer, cigarette smoke. It was immediately evident that Catherine had been here recently, for the flat was tidier than usual. The piles of old weeklies were stacked neatly beside the sideboard which, though cluttered with Mrs Cornelius's cryptic souvenirs, lacked the bottles, cans and empty packages she allowed to accumulate while her daughter was not in residence. Mrs Cornelius made for the gas-stove in the far corner, picked up the dented kettle and filled it at the tap over the sink. Una could see through to Mrs Cornelius's small, dark bedroom, with its huge wardrobe, its walls covered with photographs, many of them cut from magazines and newspapers. The other door was shut. This was the door to Catherine's room.

'She's not up yet, lazy bitch,' said Mrs Cornelius. 'Cuppa tea?' She had relaxed and was friendly. Of her children's acquaintances Una was one of the few Mrs Cornelius actually liked. It did not stop Una being afraid of the woman as of nobody else.

'Thanks.' Una hated the prospect.

Mrs Cornelius shuffled to her daughter's door and hammered on it. 'Wakey, wakey, rise an' shine. 'Ere's yer mate fer yer!'

'What?' It was Catherine.

Mrs Cornelius laughed. 'It'd take the 'Orn o' Fate ter get 'er up!'

Suddenly the whole flat smelled of rose water. It was wonderful; a miracle.

'Bugger,' said Mrs Cornelius, picking up the fallen bottle.

VII

She found Lobkowitz where she had last met him, in the ruined auditorium. Through the speakers of an inefficient tannoy came the familiar last passages of the *Browning Overture*. Then there was silence.

'Browning was a prose Wagner and so was Ives,' said the Prinz as he dusted down his tweed fishing suit.

'You've been seeing Cornelius. Is he back?'

'With a vengeance.'

'Anything I'd recognise.'

'You know his penchants ...'

'I'm not surprised, though I felt he'd crack.'

Prinz Lobkowitz seemed to tire of this exchange. He leaned against the warped piano. 'There's rarely any danger of that. He just goes dormant.'

'I was right to trust my instincts, then?'

'Always, Una.'

'They're so hard to rationalise.'

'We waste too much time trying to produce quick resolutions, when usually they're on the way and we don't know it.'

She was amused. 'The voice of experience!'

'I hope so.'

'Anyway, he's better?'

'Yes, he's better. The usual fever. We all suffer from it.'

She was not sure this was true of her, but she said: 'I was never any good at instant decisions.'

'Maybe because you had more to lose than anybody else.'

She shrugged.

'Anyway,' he continued wistfully, 'you received his message?'

'It was unmistakeable.'

'You didn't have to fulfil all his obligations. He was grateful when he heard.'

'There were other people involved. It wasn't his ego I was worried about. He was stupid to have tried for the Presidency. Then, of all times! He was never what you'd call a convinced republican, or a democrat, in the accepted sense.'

'Surely, though, that's why he tried?'

She nodded. 'I'm glad America's pulled a couple of decent chestnuts out of the fire.'

'You couldn't say they deserved it. But I'm sentimental about George Washington, too. Chile, Brazil, the Argentine – their worst crime was a kind of naive complacency. Admittedly that attitude leads to excesses of brutality in the long run.' Lobkowitz yawned. 'I've never seen so much jungle on fire. And whole mountains. The apocalypse. I wish you'd been here.'

'I had to go back to England.'

'I know.' He was sympathetic. He put a white hand on her shoulder. 'Will you stay for a while now? In New England? You have a place in the Appallachians, haven't you?'

'A couple, at different ends. But there's a sub-tenant in one. He must have been there forty years or more. It would be interesting to see how he's getting on. I haven't aged that much. Not superficially.'

He shook his head. 'You can be very vague at times. Feminine, eh?'

'Is that what it is?' She bent to kiss his hand. 'Have you got the map? I'd better get going.'

VIII

'You're still looking ill.' She tried to disguise any hint of sympathy. She forced her mouth into disapproving lines.

'They don't treat you very well. But I'm grateful, really. It kept me out of the war. I always wondered how I'd do it.'

'You thought you could stop it. You remember?'

He was bashful. 'Oh, yes. So thanks again.'

All his old charm had returned and it was hard for her not to warm to him, as she had first warmed, long ago. The self-pity was gone, for the moment, and he had a good deal of his old style. He fingered the collar of his black car coat, turning the lapels so that they framed his pale face. 'It's cold for spring.'

'The long range forecasts are predicting an Ice Age again.'

'Always a bad psychological sign. And the computers?'

'That we'll all be dead in a year or two.'

He grinned. 'Acute depression often follows a period of frenetic activity. You'll see – in a few months the weather forecasts will give us brilliant summers, plenty of rain for the crops, mild winters, and the computers will be going on about a Golden Age.' He put his arm around her shoulders. It was awful how quickly her resolutions disappeared. Her struggle lasted less than a second. 'Stick with me, baby,' he promised, 'and it will always be a golden age somewhere.'

'That's not what you were saying the last time we spoke,' she reminded him.

'We all suffer from depression occasionally.' He dismissed the creature he had been. Probably he didn't remember. She began to think that his attitude was the healthiest.

She climbed into the driving seat of the Rambler. He sat beside her, watching her with approval as she started the big car. 'It's a good thing petrol's cheap again. Where are we going? Concord?'

'Yes. First.' As she started the engine the tape she had been playing came on. He reached to remove it. 'Enough of that classical stuff,' he said. 'Let's have something romantic and jolly.' He sorted through the box of cartridges on the seat between them. 'Here we are.'

He slotted the *Holiday Symphony* into the player. 'Much better.'

He leaned back in the car as she drove it down the bumpy track to the empty highway.

'That's what I like about you, Una. You know how to relax.'

The world's most experienced airline.